just play

The Simple Truth Behind
Musical Excellence

NICK BOTTINI

RETHINK PRESS

First published in Great Britain 2018
by Rethink Press (www.rethinkpress.com)

© Copyright Nick Bottini

Cover design by Emir Orucevic (www.studiopulp.net)

just play

'We have assumed for too long that the idea of obtaining 'peak performance' pertains to those particularly in the world of sport or music performance. However, it is becoming increasingly clear that many of us wish to tap into the so-called secrets of high-level consistency throughout many aspects of our daily lives, as more and more juggling has to be negotiated within our 24-hour day. As a professional musician myself, whereby expectancy, habit and attitude form vital ingredients of high-level performance, one aspect that is crucial and relevant to us all is to listen to ourselves within the moment we are living. Listening is about clarity in focus and concentration. Listening is paying attention. I avoid being hostage to systems, methods or rituals that clog my mind and body. Listening to and respecting the purring of my engine is a vital part in adapting. Nick Bottini has given us the opportunity through *Just Play* to examine the prospect of shedding all that often burdens our mind and body; to truly celebrate in the fact that we can all achieve heights beyond what we thought possible through allowing the mind to clear, the system to empty, and the clarity and flow of listening to create a journey we may not have thought possible.'

DAME EVELYN GLENNIE, three-time Grammy award-winner, pioneering solo percussionist, and jewellery designer

'Nick has written a book that will help musicians to finally get out of their own way and unlock their full potential.'

BILL LAURANCE, pianist and keyboardist in three-time Grammy award-winning band *Snarky Puppy*

'This is a game changer, not only for musicians but for all of us.'

CHRIS WILLIAMS, saxophonist with Mercury Prize-nominated band *Led Bib*

'This really is a remarkable book. Nick gives a most splendid and erudite explanation of the creative process and the route toward excellence. I recommend it to anyone wishing to learn how to achieve greatness in any field whilst overcoming the largest of obstacles possible... our own thoughts.'

NIGEL HITCHCOCK, session saxophonist (Ray Charles, Robbie Williams, Tom Jones, Mark Knopfler, Take That, Jamiroquai, Spice Girls) and member of *Itchy Fingers*

'Whoever you are, and whatever your connection to music, you will find this book is a treasure trove of insight. It integrates the deepest and most vital elements of humanity, enables the reader to stop overthinking, and, instead, to reconnect with a profound sense of freedom and spontaneity.'

SUSAN COLLIER, Junior Academy violin professor at the Royal Academy of Music, London

'I've known Nick Bottini a long time, and his revolutionary approach to music coaching is sorely needed in the music industry. *Just Play* is a gem of a book that shows you how to stop struggling and start thriving. Buy it!'

STEPHEN ASAMOAH-DUAH, 2011 winner of the UK Young Drummer of the Year competition, and member of the Mercury prize-nominated band *The Compozers*

'Thanks to Nick, I saw for myself that 'chasing the zone' really is chasing your own tail. This book explains how and why that is, and that not only is there little point in chasing it, there's no need. And I find that in that space of understanding, the good stuff just happens.'

MICHAEL YOUNG, Prize-winning conductor, artistic director of the *Beethoven Orchestra for Humanity*, and assistant conductor of the *English Symphony Orchestra*

'Nick is a revolutionary with an incredibly clear and powerful insight into how we function as human beings. If you take your time with this book, you'll get more than you expect. I'm a much happier and sanguine musician for it.'

DAVID LALE, Cellist, *London Philharmonic Orchestra*

'Nick beautifully points us towards a simple and yet powerful understanding, which will help musicians the world over. What deeper joy than to remember again our innate potential, to reconnect to life and music making with greater clarity, passion and presence. Dive into this book with an open mind and 'just play' with the journey that is being a creative human being.'

ILDIKÓ ALLEN, Soprano, (*BBC Singers, The Sixteen, London Voices, RSVP Voices*) singing teacher, and coach

'Finally, a book applying the Three Principles to music! Two of my biggest loves. By looking way behind the curtain of the 'flow' experience and what keeps people from experiencing it, Nick Bottini takes a new, completely different, more penetrating and refreshing approach than do other musical coaches to get at the very heart of how any musician or aspiring musician – and, really, any athlete, artist or writer – can see beyond themselves, get out of their own way and thrive. I highly recommend this book to anyone who plays or aspires to play music professionally or just for fun. And that goes for artists, writers and athletes, too.'

DR JACK PRANSKY, author of *Somebody Should Have Told Us!* and *Seduced by Consciousness*

'In *Just Play*, Nick Bottini brilliantly spotlights the simple truth behind musical excellence … flourishing mental health is our most natural state … always poised to 'bubble-up' and masterfully conduct the symphony of our thinking. Get in touch with your inner music, and start playing in tune with the life you are composing in each moment.'

DR TOM KELLEY, Licensed Psychologist, Professor, Wayne State University, Author of *How Good Can You Stand It?*

'Nick has a fundamental message, not just for musicians but for people from all walks of life, about where our experiences truly come from. Although we convince ourselves that we are the ones playing, be it an instrument or the game of life, and need to control our psychological wellbeing and mindset, there is something deeper at play. Nick shares this beautifully in this book packed with nuggets of wisdom.'

DR RANI BORA, Holistic Psychiatrist, Resilience coach, speaker, Author of *How to Turn Stress On Its Head – The Simple Truth That Can Change Your Relationship With Work*

'In *Just Play*, Nick Bottini introduces musicians (and the world) to an age-old, but deeply hidden, paradigm for performance. Understanding – not grinding, pushing, or forcing – is the sole key to both passion and excellence. This book is designed to activate this understanding from deep within you. Savour every page.'

GARRET KRAMER, founder of Inner Sports and author of *Stillpower* and *The Path of No Resistance*

I dedicate this book
to the Music within.
May that one formless song
continue to be sung.

Contents

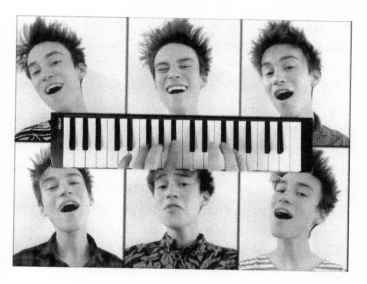

FOREWORD BY
JACOB COLLIER

We spend so much of our lives believing there is an ultimate freedom to be found. It seems the freer our minds are, the better our lives will be. Life becomes a series of circlings around those rare moments where we feel part of a 'flow' – where everything makes sense, where there are infinite possibilities, where we feel no separation between ourselves and the world around us; when we are freed from our judgements and the judgement of others. How, we often ask, can we engineer such moments? It has been a primary fascination of human beings since the dawn of literature and philosophy: to find ways to free our minds, to enhance our creative powers, and to express ourselves to the highest order.

And so, we 'play'. Some of us play musically. Music is a fundamental part of being human; whether a listener or a creator, there is so much that can be experienced through this non-verbal expression of both emotional and intellectual frameworks. There has been a great deal of study on the subject of what makes music such a universal and powerful force, and much research has gone into the most effective ways to master the skills required to create and understand music.

As a musician, understanding one's inner world is of critical importance – much more than a set of skills. After all, it's not a skill set that creates a musician; it's the decisions he is able to make with those skills. This is why, so often, very young children who are barely able to string a sentence together can come out with the most profound nuggets of wisdom. As Miles Davis famously said, 'Anybody can play. The note is only twenty percent. The attitude of the motherfucker who plays it is eighty percent'.

In musical education, so often are we told to focus on the 'external' world of learning – to focus on music as a physical process: muscle memory, hours of repetitive motion, memorising passages, operating within concrete theoretical frameworks, reading and writing, judging things as good and bad, right and wrong; master-student hierarchies; the long road from *here* to *there*. For a small number of musicians, this intellectual way of learning appears to be effective. For many others, myself included, this way of learning simply doesn't chime.

In my family home in London, there is a magical room filled with musical instruments. It's always been that way. As a two-year-old, I used to sit on my mother's lap in this room and watch as she taught the violin to her students. Not only did I find myself drinking in the magic of the music she was making, but I also watched the way she drew the music out of each individual – the love, energy, wisdom and gentleness with which she communicated ideas – and the time she took to get to know each individual person, to learn how they worked and what they were fed by, to draw the music out of them. This was at the same time in my life as I was learning to talk. Music, it seemed, was something within everybody. I was hooked.

It was in this room that I first experienced a state of play. And by 'play', I mean the grandest, most majestic kind of play – being a child, creating in a child's world. Whatever I imagined to be true, was true. I had a space in which to be; to experiment, to listen, to examine, to try things out – all for no particular reason. I followed anything that tickled my fancy, just because it tickled my fancy.

Looking back, I found myself creating before I

could decide whether creating would be a good idea or not. I reflect on the many hours, days, weeks, months, years I have spent (and continue to spend) in this room (the room in which I write these words), and never do I feel like I was straining to get somewhere in particular ... I simply loved to play. Those *zing* moments, those chords that make my eyes widen, rhythms that made my toes wiggle, sounds that make the goosebumps cascade down one or both of my arms ... I wanted to chase them. Why, when I sing *this* note in *this* chord, does it create such warmth? Why, when I take *this* note away, does it maintain its motion but leave me wanting more? I sought to get right to the heart of those sounds, and to be 'free' with them.

To learn the language of those sounds, I realised I needed to more fully understand how the different elements of music fitted together, and, as with any language, the best way to learn was to get started 'speaking' it. Using the things around me, I began to build and experiment far and wide with different musical sounds. First, I used my voice to illustrate as much as I could, and soon afterwards I gravitated towards the piano, wherein lay all manner of intriguing sounds, which, when combined, gave me chords and harmony. I began multi-track recording on a musical recording software called Cubase at the age of seven and switched over to Logic (another recording software platform) at the age of eleven. In a profoundly 21st-century way, this gave all the freedom in the world. With a microphone and an ignited imagination, I founded a world of my own – I could combine and invent using the sounds around me together in whichever way I pleased.

This was my learning process. I thought of myself as a sort of sound architect. It didn't matter where the sounds came from; if something made a sound, it had value. What would happen, I wondered, if I combined the sound of a saucepan-knock, two finger snaps panned left and right, a knee tap and a castanet, and used the combined sound in place of a traditional 'clap' sound in a song, for example? I gradually collected more and more recipes for unusual and emotional ways of using musical ideas – using sounds that sounded like my life, like my childhood home, that meant things to me. Gradually, I gravitated towards new instruments: from the left hand of the piano, I discovered the bass, from which I found the guitar, and from there the mandolin, the ukulele, etc Every time I picked up a new instrument, I felt like I was speaking another dialect of the same language – I was learning new ways to be 'at play' with each instrument, and thus learning more about how music could be experienced from every angle. I didn't think to take myself seriously – I was too busy creating. I experimented with music as a toddler does with new words as they are learning them – stringing sentences together, clumsily at first, out of the 'words' and 'phrases' I was gathering from all the listening and experimenting I was doing, combining the things I knew in new ways.

This, I suppose, could be clocked up and quanti-
fied as hours upon hours of practice, but in reality, it
felt like far from that. Without teachers to guide me,
I was following my feet. By no means was it always
straightforward; working alone, as an uncompromising
perfectionist, I'd often run into creative black holes, or
end up chasing an idea around my head until I lost
it in the quagmire of overthought. The more music I
played, the more I realised that so much of the learning
process is about understanding the inner workings of
the mind. I was (and remain) fascinated, intrigued,
frustrated and in awe, constantly, of how unpredictable
and powerful the mind can be.

In the last few years, I've become increasingly
interested in this, and my searchings led me to many
new places, such as the world of Classical Chinese
Medicine and the work of luminary authors like Syd
Banks. Such thinkers discussed the formless aspects
of creating, thinking and living, with an elegance
and effortlessness I had never encountered before.
Their ideas seemed to be disarmingly simple. A lot of
their philosophies were inverse to traditional methods
of understanding, and seemed almost illogical, but
simultaneously made all the sense in the world. A
lot was more to do with 'trusting' than engaging any
kind of effort. I realised that there was a whole new
world of thinking that seemed to be emerging, where
the primary portion of learning happened not in the
'information' part of the brain but in the 'intuition'

part – and that a marriage between these two can be not only possible but magnificent.

In your hands, you hold a book written by a musician for musicians, on the matter of mind. In my opinion, such a book has been a long time coming. Is there a secret recipe for achieving a state of play? Of course not. Another book claiming to provide such a solution wouldn't be worth your time. Here is someone who understands the nature of universal principles; who has a deep enough understanding not to impose them upon you. As Nick Bottini so eloquently puts it, 'nothing is ever truly taught, only ever learnt'. Who better to make the decisions about how you want to learn than you?

There are many treasures to be found in this book – I am certain you will enjoy plucking them out for yourself. I hope you will begin to feel more acquainted with your inner world; empowered to acknowledge and forgive all the various whirrings of the mind, for simply being itself; and to more deeply enjoy the simple, glorious nature of being alive as a human being. After all, it's all rather wonderful.

Enjoy, and go play!

AUTHOR'S NOTE

This book is about a paradigm shift in performance psychology, so some of the ways we have traditionally thought about the mind will be brought into question, and the words we routinely use may need to be reconsidered. Throughout this book, you will find that I use three words in a specific, but unconventional, way. Each is presented here as a psychological *principle* – an immutable law that explains how the mind truly works. Only an undergirding principle can actually represent how a domain truly functions. Please take care and refer back to this list and reflect on these principles whenever you need to.

(The Principle of Universal) THOUGHT – the spiritual 'energy' that generates all aspects of reality. This creative agent is the sole source of all psychological experience.

(The Principle of Universal) MIND – The interconnectedness of all things. The intelligence of life, or of Mother Nature. The one being that we all share.

(The Principle of Universal) CONSCIOUSNESS – the fact of awareness, and that this awareness is universal. This is the only place that experience exists.

When I am specifically talking about the principle, rather than merely using the word, the term will be formatted in the style denoted above – in other words, for example, THOUGHT (the principle) vs. thought (the term as it is commonly used).

Though these principles are presented as three for the sake of clarity, it is not because they are truly separate from each other. It may be helpful to think of them as facets of the same gemstone.

ACKNOWLEDGEMENTS

It takes the love of many people to write a book. First, I am grateful for my countless teachers: my mother and father, who taught me what music was; my sisters and wider family with whom I first discovered I could *play*; my beloved school teacher, Slim Hopgood, for seeing the light in me and coaxing it out. I'm of course blessed by the numerous teachers who have shown me the how and the what, and who have taken many forms – colleagues, students, clients and critics. My sincere gratitude to all those who read the manuscript at various stages and offered invaluable suggestions.

Next, to my coaches: Jamie Smart – thank you for introducing me to the legacy of Syd Banks and for showing me I was, in fact, an author. Garret Kramer – I'm astounded by the clarity and relentlessness with which you point me back to truth and love. Special thanks to my editor Joel Drazner for his saintly patience and never-ending good humour. I would also like to thank Damian Mark Smyth for helping me get the project rolling, and the folks at Rethink Press for helping me complete it. Enormous thanks to all the backers of the Kickstarter campaign that allowed the project to launch in the way that it has (with special mention to Kimberley Hare, Sophia Katerinis, Sean Burgess, Nicky Gentil, Amir Karkouti, Tim Gunner, Kayll Frappier, Lewis Buxton, Alan Duguid, Lori Carpenos, Susan Ann Hills, Debra Simmons, Marina Galan, and Joe Gregory).

Finally, I would like to thank my beautiful wife, Polina – my Russian princess. I'm afraid I will always be your 'crazy Englishman'.

ONE

LET'S START AT THE VERY BEGINNING

When I first started writing *Just Play*, I was jet-lagged, returning to the UK after visiting my wife's family near Yekaterinburg in west Central Russia. Although I'm a musician, I had the idea of running the title past a professional footballer friend named Lewis Buxton. Soon after I'd told him that I was writing a book about music, performance and the mind, he messaged me in the middle of the night. My iPhone buzzed, and it illuminated the overheated hotel room. In the message, Lewis told me that he used to visit Emma, a sports psychologist in Manchester, because both when he was playing, and more generally, he had been having the feeling that he was missing something. Lewis told me that although the sessions did help, before long he would be struggling again. Emma would ask him to close his eyes and recall a time when he'd felt confident. He said he would always go back to the same

time, age twelve, and she would ask him to describe
how he felt:

> I would say, 'I feel... free, cocky almost, confident,
> fearless, a step ahead, *in the flow!*' Then Emma
> would say, 'If you could give some advice to your
> grown-up self, what would it be?' The answer was
> always the same...
> 'Just play!'
> 'Just go and play!'

I stood there in my birthday suit at 3am, wide
awake, not really knowing where I was. The similarities
between his story and my own were striking. The kind
of inner struggles that Lewis and I both experienced
are universal and are not unique to music or sport. The
principles I'm going to share in this book apply to all
of us, regardless of whether you call yourself a musician, because they encapsulate a deeper truth about
the human condition. The truth is that it is always
possible to have an effortless relationship with music,
and with life itself. Whatever complications we have
conjured up, we are always free to let go of them. This
is because much like the body has an immune system,
the mind has one, too. This spiritual immune system
is the missing link in psychology that the science of
expertise has mostly overlooked, and this system is
the basis of our innate ability to create, flourish and
master a craft.

The Missing Link In Performance Psychology

In its youth, the field of psychology set out to understand the *psyche*, or the soul, but in trying to become more 'scientific' and less 'spiritual', it has tended to focus predominantly on the study of behaviour and biology. Over the last thirty years or so, psychologists, music teachers, coaches, motivational speakers, self-help authors and even film directors have massaged ideas into the collective conscious that are much like 'The Emperor's New Clothes'. Many ideas about the mind are very seductive and widely taught, but closer inspection reveals they have been built on shaky ground. Although there has been growing interest in the study of expert performance, this whole field, much like psychology itself, is based on some fairly hefty, rarely questioned assumptions.

The most fundamental of these assumptions is the idea that by reapplying the *behaviours, habits or techniques* of high performers, we can simply reverse-engineer human excellence from the outside-in. There is a tacit assumption that the 'outputs' of high performers (states of mind, methods, practice regimes, or decisions, etc) can be adopted as 'inputs' with which we can reliably duplicate high-level results. This belief comes about because we like to think the mind functions like a machine. This is why it's so common to hear computer analogies like 'reprogramming' the mind, or flow 'hacking', implying that is possible for our mental 'software' to be worked around or changed at will. But while there may appear to be similarities, as we shall see, fundamentally the two are *not* alike. The power of the mind lies in exactly that which distinguishes us from machines – in the very fact that we are alive.

The Simple Truth – Correlation vs. Causation

In this book, I will be asking you to put what you already know about the mind on hold and consider something new but strangely familiar. To set the scene for this new psychology, let's take a parallel example from the history of medicine.

In the 1840s, most people believed that disease was caused by bad air, or 'miasmas'. Historically, they would open windows to let the miasmas escape, and they carried posies of flowers to ward off bad smells, but because germs weren't part of their understanding of how infection spread, they would rarely wash their hands. No one realised the need. It wasn't even required for surgeons to scrub up or sterilise their implements before operating on patients. From a modern perspective, this may seem irresponsible, but the surgeons innocently used their contaminated implements because they didn't know about the underlying principles behind the spread of disease. Such principles had yet to be discovered by Ignaz Semelweiss and proven by Louis Pasteur. As with the 'programming theory' of the human mind, there were several grains of truth that supported the miasma misunderstanding of disease, such as:

1. It was observable that disease *could* be spread.

2. Bad smells often accompany disease, death and decay.

3. We are naturally repelled by bad smells, and even instinctively avoid eating food that smells spoiled. [This, by the way, has an evolutionary purpose.]

The problem with the miasma theory, however, was that it was possible for a surgeon's scalpel to be covered in bacteria, without any noticeable smell. It was also possible for a room to smell unpleasant, but for the people in it to be healthy and uninfected. The simple truth was that there was a lurking variable – germs. The key distinction was between **correlation** – (two factors occurring at the same time), and **causation** (one factor precipitating the other, or causing it). When correlation is mistaken for causation, you end up with a rule of thumb rather than an immutable law, and you get bad science rather than truth. What this seemingly tiny oversight caused in the 1840s was chaos and undue suffering on a grand scale. Moreover, in the hospital where Semelweiss was working, doctors were involved in autopsies but were not sterilising their hands or scalpels before touching living patients. The very doctors who were supposed to be helping were actually killing patients by spreading disease significantly faster than by their midwife colleagues, who were not performing autopsies.

Just as a misunderstanding of disease caused doctors to inadvertently harm the patients they were trying to help, the same could be said of sports psychologists, coaches and music teachers promoting the world's most widespread misunderstanding of the mind to their students and clients. Sadly, misunderstanding the mind can actually result in no less grave consequences than ignorance of germs had caused in the 1840s.

CORRELATION	CAUSATION
A happens at the same time as B	A causes B
A seems to cause B	A genuinely causes B

The reason that ideas like mind programming or flow hacking can endure is that we easily notice *correlation*, while the subtly hidden *cause* goes unnoticed. Just like with the miasma theory, there are grains of truth that seem to support the ideas, but we are not actually experiencing *causation* the way we can think we are. Today, much like the misinformed doctors of the 19th century, we innocently draw the best conclusions we can, given our current level of understanding. But we end up reaching a conclusion that has anomalies, while the truth of the matter remains hidden.

For example, often when people notice that a so-called mindset technique isn't working, they end up believing that it must be *them*, or perhaps their therapist, who is misapplying the technique. By 'techniques', I'm referring to approaches as varied as Neuro-Linguistic Programming (NLP), Cognitive Behavioural Therapy (CBT), hypnosis, meditation, mindfulness, breathing techniques – in fact – any external or internal intervention applied with the intention of deliberately changing a person's state of mind. Let me be clear – if you have been using these approaches, I'm not suggesting that you stop. And I'm not advising anyone against trying them, either. I'm simply inviting you to get clear for yourself about what really causes our thoughts and moods to change when they do. Is it really a 'technique' or something else – a lurking variable? When I first became interested in the mental aspects of performance, it didn't even cross my mind that the relaxation and visualisation techniques I was trying to use might be imposters. Why would it? These kinds of techniques were everywhere – all over the Internet, in films, taught in schools, even. Sometimes when I followed the techniques, they seemed to work brilliantly, but the problem was that at other times there was absolutely no impact, and worse, I ended up trying to figure out what I had done wrong. Why didn't they always work? This in itself, however, was never enough for me to question the techniques themselves. In much the same way that germs were the missing link for the medical patients of the 1840s, the simple truth remaining largely unnoticed today is the spiritual nature of the mind. When we stop resisting our own thoughts, feelings and perceptions, everything gets simpler.

A Matter Of Principle

In the 1890s, when psychology was still an emerging science, William James, an influential pioneer, foresaw a serious problem for the new field. In *Psychology: The Briefer Course*, written in 1892, he clearly spelled out the state of disarray. He warned his colleagues not to assume that psychology stood at last 'on solid ground', because all he saw being reported were strings of raw facts from stabs in the dark rather than genuine scientific insight into how the mind works. This was because no one had discovered any laws, or *principles*, underpinning the whole science:

> But at present psychology is in the condition of physics before Galileo and the laws of motion, of chemistry before Lavoisier and the notion that mass is preserved in all reactions. The Galileo and the Lavoisier of psychology will be famous men indeed when they come, and come they some day surely will...

After reading this, some of his colleagues went on to compare themselves to Galileo and Lavoisier, but in truth, as we shall see, the lawless state of psychology remained virtually unchallenged for most of the following century. James predicted that the discovery of the undergirding principles of psychology would be as significant to humankind as the discovery of fire, but today, at the time of this writing, the thought revolution has only just begun. Exploring this tide change fully is beyond the scope of this book, but suffice it to say that an insight first articulated in the 1970s in Canada not only heralds an exciting new chapter in the study of excellence, but also bridges the gap between traditional psychology and spirituality. Today, not only posies and miasmas are obsolete; positive thinking and willpower have also had their time. It's now time to simplify our relationship with the mind, and in turn, with music. This book is about getting to the beating heart of excellence and the true underlying principles behind it, rather than making stabs in the dark that only partially correlate.

From the outset, I want to reassure you that, no matter what you may think about yourself, no matter your previous musical training, past experiences, or current situation, you never actually lost touch with your musical inner child. Passion, creativity, and excellence are your birthright, and understanding how excellence works is the key to accessing those qualities more of the time. Although I am a musician, this is not a book about music. I will draw on musical examples and stories from my own life, but music is not really the point here. It is about something far bigger, the nature and origin of all human excellence and what gets in the way of achieving it. This is a matter of how all minds work, not just those of high performers, and how an understanding of simplicity can have a profoundly transformative effect, not just in music, or in sport, but in your whole life. That said, however, stick with it. As Galileo or Semelweiss would have told you, true paradigm shifts are usually met with mixed reactions, to say the least. So give yourself time. Read this book as slowly as you need to, and perhaps even slower than that. This is not a job for the intellect.

Reading With A Beginner's Mind

Deeply understanding the principles in this book will have a transformative effect not only on your music but on your life as a whole. That said, to help you to get the most from this book, I invite you to embark on reading *Just Play* with a child's openness and as a total beginner – with a mind like a *tabula rasa*.

Zen teacher Shunryu Suzuki said: "In the beginner's mind there are many possibilities, but in the expert's there are few." He was referring to how the openness of a beginner's mind is their greatest asset. The fact is it's yours, too. Flirt with the possibility that there may be something profound waiting to be uncovered, and also that it could be hiding in a terrain that you thought you knew like the back of your hand, in the place you least expect it. Be prepared to explore the familiar, but with a fresh curiosity. You may also be surprised by what happens as you re-read the book after you have explored it the first time – kind of like discovering several books in one!

Rather than reading quickly to confirm what you already know, I invite you to read in a way that affords you the space to be struck by insights. 'Eureka' moments seem to come out of nowhere, and they usually arrive when we least expect them, not when we are striving or resisting. In fact, getting the most out of this book has a lot more to do with giving up 'the known' than it has to do with learning anything new. It's not that we will come to intellectually understand about germs but carry a posy of flowers 'just in case'. Instead, as soon as we are struck by an insight, it will forever stop making sense to act superstitiously. Our actions change by implication – it's not a matter of practice. I suppose you could call this the difference between head learning and heart learning. Suddenly the world just seems different, and because of that, new possibilities open up.

Although they may have been interested in reading one, the doctors of the 1840s didn't need a book about the most effective posy-making methods, new investigations into bloodletting or 'The Six Top Tips To Prolong the Life of Your Scalpel Blade'. They needed light shining on the unknown variable – germs. In the same way, you will neither find a chapter about visualisation nor a formula for a positive mental attitude or achieving the mindset of excellence. Instead, you will find my best attempt to shine light on something that has been lurking in the background – the counterintuitive way that the mind works. Just like the new paradigm of disease, understanding the nature of THOUGHT will clear up many a mystery and dramatically increase the likelihood of flourishing in any field, be it sport, work, business, relationships, or music.

Let the show commence...

TWO

GO WITH THE FLOW

Flow has become a hot topic in psychological research in recent years, but it's a relatively new field, especially within the domain of music. Despite psychologists piecing together their ideas about the nature of flow, it remains an area with a great many unanswered questions – particularly about the anomalies to some of the most popular theories. That said, something about flow seems universally attractive to us. Sportspeople or business people might refer to being 'in the zone'. Jazz or popular musicians might speak about being 'in the groove'. We might say we 'lose ourselves' in an activity. Buddhists, similarly, might talk about a state of 'no mind' – jhāna – or of meditation. Experiences of flow are often described as uplifting, life-affirming, even transcendent. Whatever the endeavour – be it golf, painting, work, playing the cello, public speaking or just about anything – flow experiences are typically reported as being so enjoyable that participants want to go back for more. Given how wonderful flow can be, it seems logical to ask: 'What can I do to get back there?' 'How do I teach it?' 'How do I stay there?' But trying to do anything to achieve flow or to teach it is problematic. The fact that we even ask such questions in the first place is based on a misunderstanding of how the mind works.

What if most people's efforts to achieve flow actually take them further from it? What if well-meaning parents, psychologists, coaches, leaders, therapists and teachers are innocently teaching us to buy into a common illusion, a misunderstanding that gets in every musician's way? In fact, it's the one misunderstanding that gets in everyone's way. A trick of the mind that, once appreciated deeply for what it truly is, will set you free and will finally fill in the missing piece in the puzzle of flow.

'Flow' Is Only Half The Story

When you ask high performers in any field what they are thinking about when they experience flow, very often they can't give you much detail. And there's a very good reason for this. What they are being asked to recall are precisely the moments when they barely notice their thoughts at all, because they have a clear head. When the experience is flowing, we can be fully absorbed in the moment and lose all sense of self. Now, by contrast, if you ask people to tell you about the times when they haven't been in the zone, there is usually a lot more to say: they are more self-conscious, more likely to perceive limitations, and, in general, they are more inclined to notice their thoughts and their inner monologue.

These observations point to the first simple truth about flow:

SIMPLE TRUTH NO. 1:
THOUGHTS JUST COME AND GO.

When the mind clears, we find ourselves in flow. When it fills up with thoughts, we drag ourselves out of flow. This filling and emptying is the natural play of the mind. Awareness ebbs and flows, and this is all normal and healthy, whatever your state of mind in the moment. Ebb and flow happen to absolutely everyone.

Although awareness may seem like a mystical word, all I am pointing to here is the fact is that our mood, our emotional condition, our state of mind, our head space – whatever you want to call it – ebbs and flows on its own. Both the ebb and the flow are healthy, and essential. So you can see that although it might feel logical to ask, 'How do I get into the zone?', such inquiry requires that you assume three things:

1. That one state of mind is better than another.
2. That there is something that you can do to get there.
3. That flow is something that doesn't just happen on its own.

But none of these assumptions are actually true. The mind is naturally clear, and it is naturally prone to clouding over – like crystal-clear water with sediment in it. Cloudy isn't worse than clear per se, it merely tells you which state the water's in. The world seems different of course when viewed through a cloudy mind, but, because its natural state is clarity, just as it always has done, it will settle on its own.

Appearances can be deceptive, though. When a performer really moves us, it can be easy to assume that we know what's going on inside their head. Just because the listener is having a transcendental experience, however, doesn't mean the performer is. Also, the zone will come and go from one moment to the next. Given how easily we can mistake an effect for a cause, when we see a musician, seemingly in the zone, we can think that their state of mind has come from how skilled they are. It can very easily look like the performer has some special mental gift. Obviously there is a place for acquiring musical skill, but mastery doesn't cause a state of mind. Neither does individual genius. It works the other way round. It's the clearing mind that causes those effects to be revealed.

Admittedly, this might not seem so poetic, but the zone is actually a very run-of-the-mill phenomenon and nothing to do with performance at all. Just as elite performers have a hard time remembering what they were thinking while in the zone, you probably don't notice the times when you are in flow as you brush your teeth, walk, drive your car, play a computer game, have a conversation, or any of the other times it happens. Sometimes our head clears, and we are at one with the present moment; other times, we think ourselves out of it. Sometimes we lose ourselves in an activity, whereas at other times we take things personally. These are all different ways of saying that thoughts come and go on their own, regardless of who we are, or what we are doing. In this respect, we are all united.

You Can't Clear Your Head By Adding More Thinking

So if the times we experience flow are actually when we have nothing on our mind, it follows that adding more thoughts into the equation could be bad for business. Yet, that's exactly what each of us do from time to time. When most of the clients I coach first hear that getting into the zone is all about having a clear head, they think that this is a mental skill to be mastered. I can understand why, because this idea is everywhere. Whether it's visualisation, meditation, mindfulness, NLP, CBT, or hypnosis, there are still plenty of experts teaching mindset strategies as if they were tools in a required/mandatory toolkit. Ultimately, however, no such tools exist. While it's definitely possible to meddle (by trying to control certain thoughts), the mind cannot be hacked, and it doesn't need to be. Mental engineering is a nice idea that even seems to work sometimes, especially if pleasant thoughts naturally spring up while employing the 'techniques', but in the long term it's unhelpful. The zone is categorically not a mental skill to be mastered, and there is definitely no 'inner game' to be 'won', not least because the zone is no more a 'win' than any other form of emotional weather. From certain states of mind, it can seem, at times, like we are 'losing', but, in reality, whenever we try to mentally cope or control, we are only resisting the self-clearing system. Using willpower or mental techniques to achieve clarity is like trying various stirring techniques to clear the muddy water. The system only works one way. Let it be or you'll be working against it.

> **SIMPLE TRUTH NO. 2: YOU CAN'T FORCE FLOW.**
>
> The mind is a self-clearing system that you're not in charge of. All thoughts and emotions happen spontaneously, and they are neither triggered nor chosen. This spontaneity only ever follows the logic of the system; the mind is nobody's slave.

It's essential to understand that flow is not a destination to get to, and ebb is not something to fix or avoid. Flow isn't achieved through striving or overthinking. It is a natural, default state of mind that everybody experiences, and so is ebb. Psychologically, human beings are continually swinging between ebb and flow – between moments of overthinking and clear-headedness. Between an external or internal direction to our focus. Between clutter and clarity. It's extremely helpful, as we shall see, to recognise that the states of both ebb and flow are totally normal. Understanding this means that we stop trying to fix our feelings.

> **SIMPLE TRUTH NO. 3: YOU ARE THE ZONE.**
>
> You don't actually lose your 'self' in a performance. You only lose a character you thought up. And as that character dissolves, you fall back into the true self – pure universal awareness.

This third point has perhaps the most far-reaching implications – you are not your thoughts, you are that which thinks!

The zone, just like the entirety of our psychological experience, is THOUGHT-generated. By this, I'm not just referring to the act of thinking about something, which is how we often use the word. That's only a fraction of what the principle of THOUGHT actually does – it's the necessary creative agent with which we are able to construct a reality in the first place. Everything we see, hear, feel, smell, and taste, as we are experiencing it, is made by THOUGHT. Nothing (and no one) exists outside of THOUGHT, and what can never be taken out of the equation is the fact that

THOUGHT is generating all perceptions, sensations, interpretations, and moment-to-moment experiencing of the world. THOUGHT, by its nature, is creative rather than responsive, and the mind therefore generates everything we take as the facts of sensory data. Rather than being like a machine that can only collect raw data from the world, the mind is more like an artist, painting a unique story.

Pure, impersonal awareness of the zone is our essential nature, and therefore we needn't worry about the fact that we simply and naturally lose sight of it sometimes. Flow can never be caused (or stopped) by anything outside ourselves, and experiencing flow is not a prerequisite for great music making, either. This is good news. It means that regardless of whether we happen to be having a zone experience, our ability to perform at our best always remains fully intact. So, too, does our wellbeing. Ebb, just like flow, is a sign of mental health. The only real challenge we face is that while behind the scenes the mind works one way, our experience will frequently convince us that it works another. The more clearly musicians see through this illusion, the more easily they flourish. Whenever we try to censor or chase a feeling or a thought, we are doing the only thing that can slow the clearing of the mind – resisting our experience. Thoughts and feelings always go together, so we can stop assuming that our feelings are feedback on our performance or on who (we think) we are. Instead, we can look to the principle of Thought as the culprit or catalyst for our current feeling state. Merely understanding this will make the emotional rollercoaster ride that is being human that much easier. As you release your grip on the idea that you should be experiencing the zone, your attention is naturally drawn back to the here and now, and more of the time you will find yourself just *living*, without creating unnecessary mental noise. Each of the simple truths outlined in this chapter are part of a new way of understanding high performance, the details of which we'll explore further in Chapter 3. The mind only ever follows nature's agenda, so, as we shall see, much more interesting than fixating on whether the experience is ebbing or flowing is seeing where that rollercoaster is taking us. Before that, though, let's look at the rollercoaster in a bit more depth and explore how it really does work the same for everyone.

Chapter 2 Summary

MYTHS about flow:

1. You perform at your best when you experience flow.
2. You can actively put yourself into 'the zone'.
3. Some people are naturally better at achieving the zone than others.
4. Certain circumstances or actions cause flow.
5. Flow can be 'mastered' or 'hacked'.
6. Flow is a unique phenomenon that distinguishes geniuses from the rest of us.
7. Not experiencing flow is a problem.
8. Your musical skill drops when you are not in flow.
9. When in flow you lose your 'self'.

TRUTHS about flow:

1. You don't need to experience flow to perform at your best. You always have that capacity.
2. Zone experiences only ever happen by themselves when the mind clears naturally.
3. The principles behind flow are the same for all of us. You have the same capacity to experience flow as anyone else.
4. There are no special circumstances or rituals that can cause flow.

5. Flow is innate, so it cannot (and need not) be mastered. It cannot be hacked because it is already perfect.

6. The zone is an everyday phenomenon that often goes unnoticed or even disregarded. But we each possess in equal measure the ability to access it.

7. A state of mind cannot be right, wrong or a problem.

8. Your musical skill is unaffected by your state of mind.

9. When in flow, the ego (the idea you are separate) dissolves, and you get a glimpse of who you truly are.

THREE

IT DON'T MEAN A THING IF IT AIN'T GOT THAT SWING

'In Buddhism, there is no place for using effort. Just be ordinary and nothing special. Eat your food, move your bowels, pass water and when you're tired go and lie down. The ignorant will laugh at me, but the wise will understand.'

Bruce Lee, in *The Tao of Jeet Kune Do*.

When I was about nine years old, I started playing the violin. One day, I arrived at the little storeroom in my primary school where my weekly lessons took place to find that my violin teacher, Mr Hardman, wasn't there. I wandered out of the makeshift teaching studio and discovered that he was down the corridor photocopying something for me. He handed me a black-and-white picture of a stern-looking figure playing the violin, deep in musical rapture.

'This is Jascha Heifetz,' he said, 'the greatest violinist that ever lived.'

The portrait made the great Russian look heroic and formidable. Today, I still have the yellowing scrap of paper, which lived on my bedroom wall until the time that I left home. Unlike my comparatively geriatric starting age, Heifetz began the violin at the tender age of three. He was an extraordinary child prodigy, and at the time of his Carnegie Hall debut in 1917 – after having fled the revolution – he caused a sensation in the violin-playing world with his technical brilliance and an emotional intensity that would amaze audiences, inspire composers, and set the gold standard for modern violin playing.

For more than half a century, he recorded prolifically, leading by example at a time when recordings were increasingly being used as a study aid. The epitome of violinistic perfection, his sound and technique were highly influential; so it is no wonder my childhood violin teacher idolised Heifetz as a god. Generations of violinists did exactly the same; and in 1920, following the violinist's London debut, George Bernard Shaw famously wrote Heifetz a letter that shared my teacher's sentiments:

> *My dear Heifetz*
> *Your recital has filled me and my wife with anxiety. If you provoke a jealous God by playing with such superhuman perfection, you will die young. I earnestly advise you to play something badly every night before*

going to bed instead of saying your prayers. No mere mortal should presume to play so faultlessly as that.
    Sincerely
    G. Bernard Shaw

I had been aware of this story, but it took me many years to fully grasp the fact that Heifetz wasn't *actually* superhuman. Although he played the violin as perfectly as anyone could have hoped for, it's easy to forget that each of Heifetz's moments of genius was a human accomplishment. We may well glimpse the divine in our musical idols, but that divinity is all part and parcel of being human. So, although others may be highly skilled, at the spiritual level there's nothing actually separating them from you or I. To the untrained eye, high performers like Heifetz may seem otherworldly, but only because we don't understand the magic. When we consider celebrities, innovators, or elite performers, we often find ourselves looking for distinctions, but, in so doing, we miss the essential connections between people.

Chapter 2 showed that 'the zone' is just one of the many experiences we will have as humans, and we will experience it of its own accord because the mind has a tendency to get out of its own way. We also saw that all thoughts, feelings and perceptions are experienced because of the principle of THOUGHT. This chapter is all about the extraordinary rollercoaster ride that THOUGHT can take us on, and how absolutely everyone's mind works this way. I never told anyone at the time, but when I was a music college student, I used to believe that I was the only one feeling nervous before a performance. I would look at other musicians and think that it would be so much easier to be them. The truth is, however, that although we can look for and seem to find plenty of superhuman examples, what we are actually encountering is other individuals who, just like us, are riding the rollercoaster that is the human experience. In this, we are truly all one.

Allowing The Mind To Be Ordinary

It's important to understand that every human being experiences fear, nervousness, anxiety, self-doubt, sadness, and insecurities of one kind or another. This is all normal. Here's the punchline though: it's also completely normal, from a low state of mind, to imagine that others *don't* feel these feelings. Anyone can believe that their emotions need changing, even though it's neither possible nor necessary. That's the illusion. As long as we imagine that there is a group of superhumans with a secret we don't have, it makes sense to try and do what they're doing. As musicians we're often told that some emotions are good (confidence, for example), and others are bad (like anxiety), but this isn't true and never has been.

Once we take it for granted that our thoughts, feelings and perceptions need managing, we tend to make the kind of 'effort' that Bruce Lee was alluding to – we judge our experience of the moment and then try to improve it *as it's happening*. This resistance to the truth of the moment gradually becomes so conditioned that we forget there is another way. We judge instead of accepting. We try to hear. We try to feel. We try to emote. We try to think. We try to concentrate. We try to play. We try to be musical. Whenever we 'try' to do something that is innate, we only get in the way of being able to do it. True, there is a place for studying the music thoroughly – learning the language, internalising sounds, memorising, repeating movements until they become second nature. But 'trying' only wastes energy.

In It Together

Even musical idols like Heifetz, although he rarely talked about it publicly, get the same feelings of self-doubt or nerves that we all get from time to time. In 1933, for example, he recalled his first encounter with live radio broadcasting:

> I remember with what fear I came before that dreadful little black box. It seemed a spy, waiting to take each sound as I played it, and send it, with no chance of recall, to a critical and unsympathetic audience. For the first minutes of playing for that first appearance before the microphone, it was a terrific ordeal. I should not want to repeat it again. I finished the concert physically exhausted.[1]

---

1. Herbert K. Axelrod (Ed.), *Heifetz*, second edition (Neptune: Paganiniana 1981). 296.

Heifetz was describing the mental exhaustion that comes about when we mistakenly believe that our feelings come from somewhere external and then try to manage them by worrying, coping or using willpower. I'd be willing to bet that it seemed to him during that session as if his feelings were coming from the microphone, the audience, or the situation. What was invisible to him in that moment was that his experiences of fear (of the 'dreadful little black box') was THOUGHT-generated, just as yours and mine are. Again, there was nothing inherently superhuman about Heifetz being able to continue playing in spite of feeling insecure. He simply fell into the outside-in illusion like we all do, yet kept playing. As he fought against his psychology, he suffered, but the audience was probably none the wiser. Sure enough, as soon as he stopped worrying about his feelings, his 'terrific ordeal' resolved itself. In the same interview, he said that the microphone later became an 'old friend'. Once again, it wasn't because he had 'mastered' his nerves – they simply stopped being an issue as he saw the situation differently. Understanding what our feelings are and what they are really trying to tell us has an absolutely crucial role to play in developing a high level of expertise.

Let's take an example. A pianist is working on a new piece and is sight-reading through the music for the first time. As he's doing so, he comes across some unfamiliar rhythms and feels insecure. He mistakenly thinks the insecure feeling is telling him about how well he sight-reads. Rather than understanding that his feelings only ever tell him about the ebb and flow of THOUGHT, he misinterprets the feeling as proof there is a problem with his ability. He might then try to cope with the feeling by avoiding sight-reading altogether, or he might worry and resolve to work harder until it changes and he feels better about himself. Either way, his misunderstanding causes extra psychological effort, because he is trying to change a feeling that doesn't need to be changed. Over time, he either neglects sight-reading because he thinks it is the reading that 'makes' him feel bad, or he fixates on practising sight-reading in an attempt to guarantee a feeling of confidence. This becomes a vicious cycle, because whatever he tries only offers temporary 'relief' from a problem he doesn't really have. He feels insecure, overthinks and then believes he has a sight-reading issue when all along he has merely had a misunderstanding. The fact that THOUGHT energy continually ebbs and flows is not a problem. Feeling insecure from time to time is normal, universal and in itself not a sign that that you need to practice more. The problem is that you attribute your feelings to something other than THOUGHT.

But what would happen if our pianist understood that his insecure feelings were only ever feedback on insecure thinking in the moment? Insightfully, he would recognise that such insecure feelings are completely normal and would likely find himself not dwelling on the issue of sight-reading but instead remember why he is learning the piece – for a recital in three weeks' time. While still feeling insecure, he would *continue to practise whatever makes sense in the moment rather than what feels good.* This is navigating by creative intuition rather than by fear. Because he understands the THOUGHT-feeling connection, he isn't disconnected so easily from his own inner urge to grow as a musician, or from the present moment. Over time, he tends to stay more present during his practice and reads much more readily because he's no longer struggling to avoid bad feelings. It may or may not make sense to him to work on sight-reading, but if he decides to make the effort, it will be because he wants to, not because he feels he has to protect or prove himself. It rarely crosses his mind anymore that he has a sight-reading issue, because now he reads regardless of how he feels, and when it makes sense to, he practises it.

Our experience naturally fluctuates moment to moment. Knowing this is the case for everybody who has ever lived prompts us to stop superstitiously searching down blind alleys for a fabled 'peak' performance state. We also stop trying to suppress bad feelings or to chase good ones.

The truth is:

• All experience works from the inside-out.

• We only ever feel our thinking.

- We have an extremely wide range of emotions, all of which are completely normal.
- It is possible to work with the system or against it.
- By understanding the system, we are less likely to waste energy on mismanaging something that isn't broken.

Figure 2.1: How the system works

OUTSIDE-IN (ILLUSION)	INSIDE-OUT (UNDERLYING PRINCIPLES)
Clutter.	Clarity.
Illusion of a separate self.	True self.
How the human experience seems to work sometimes.	How it always works.
In-the-moment thoughts, feelings and perceptions honestly seem to come from somewhere other than the principle – or spiritual energy – of THOUGHT.	All thoughts, feelings and perceptions are made by THOUGHT energy, creating a vivid experience in the present moment.
There is an illusory 'out there': circumstances, events, the body, past/future, personality, etc	There is only 'inside': inside the moment, inside the universal mind. Everything is made by the formless creative energy of THOUGHT.

OUTSIDE-IN (ILLUSION)	INSIDE-OUT (UNDERLYING PRINCIPLES)
Feelings seem to happen to a separate self. So we want to control what we think is causing them.	Feelings are simultaneously created and experienced, so there is no need to resist them.
The illusion of separation: the personal, disconnected, duality.	The reality of connection, unity, oneness, love.
Innocent misunderstanding.	The simplifying truth.
Compelling, but untrue.	True.
Transient.	Timeless.

Mood Swings: Nature's Rollercoaster

The simple psychological truth for all of us is that our mood rises and falls on its own. The creative power of THOUGHT is remarkable, but it can also trick us into believing that a low mood or high mood is somehow linked to the outside world or that our mood tells us something about who we are. But we are not our thoughts. Emotions can only come from one place – from the power of THOUGHT energy creating our reality in the moment. It's important to understand that just as flow is an everyday occurrence, so is ebb. This is not just an approximate rule of thumb that applies to most people except for a gifted few, but it is actually a principle of human psychology that cannot be bargained or negotiated with. Every person who has walked – or who will ever walk – the planet has experienced psychological ebb and flow. The details of their precise experience will definitely be different, but the way THOUGHT works is unarguably the same. For example, some will experience ebb as nerves that seem to come from an impending 'big' performance, and some will experience ebb as self-doubt that appears to result from a lack of talent. Others will feel over-whelm and attribute it to the busy schedule of their international tour. Some may feel elation and attribute it to a gig. The more the outside-in illusion is invisible to us, the more likely we are to act superstitiously and keep the system clogged. This is how nerves become stage fright, self-doubt becomes procrastination and overwhelm becomes a panic attack. It's also how pride becomes arrogance. It's natural to misattribute feel-ings to something on the outside, but the true source is only ever the inside. This is a spiritual truth that applies equally to all of us, whether or not we regard ourselves as a genius or as superhuman. We will always be tricked by the outside-in illusion (see Figure 2.1), but there's immense power in being in on the joke. This is the human experience in a nutshell.

'OK', I hear you cry, 'but surely not every feeling is caused by the mind. What if someone drops a piano on my foot?' Well, here's the thing, the body can be damaged, that much is true. But we experience that body (and any damage) through CONSCIOUSNESS, or awareness. Without CONSCIOUSNESS, there'd be no experience at all – good or bad. Our experience of the body is always changeable. This is how people sometimes fail to notice injuries until they have rescued a family member from danger, or why the body seems different in different states of mind. That's because our awareness of the body is only ever a psychological one and as soon as we are convinced that some experiences happen outside of CONSCIOUSNESS, we've gone outside-in.

As with everything I'm outlining, it's not so much about applying this understanding to avoid pain or unpleasant emotions, but rather it's about knowing what's actually going on, which gives us the best chance as performers. Natural mood changes can happen when we are performing, practising, watching other high performers, interacting with others, working, relaxing, leading, or creating. The activity itself does not determine our feelings, though it can certainly seem like it does. When we think about mood swings, especially when referring to psychiatric 'disorders', there is often an assumption that our moods are really supposed to be stable, that our psychological experience is not supposed to fluctuate. In fact, nothing could be further from the truth, and as we're about to see, it's important that our moods do fluctuate.

Who Are You, Really?

What kind of spiritual being is riding this emotional rollercoaster? You aren't a job, a personality, a body or a set of skills. You aren't your thoughts, either, so it's much deeper than that. You are the true self – you are pure awareness. The same shared universal awareness that we all are. A place of inner stillness that is the source, if you will. The place from which the best ideas and decisions come. The true self is the perceiver, not the perception. The thinker, not the thought. The music of life, not the musician. So, it doesn't really matter what shape the emotional rollercoaster takes, because it's all a creation, and all the while, the creator is always safe. Nor does it matter how often you loop the loop or how long you stay up or down for. It's all allowed. It's perfectly normal. *You're* perfectly normal. Rollercoasters are supposed to be a wild ride and so is life. Just as a violin string oscillates when life is breathed into the music, so, too, do *we* oscillate emotionally. This is how it is supposed to be. It is the natural rhythm of life.

As soon as we realise that the emotional rollercoaster is actually a universal experience, we stop dividing people into groups. There are no high performers, gurus or celebrities who know something you don't know or who have a capacity to feel continuously confident and driven in a way you and I don't experience. That's an illusion. Excellence is in your nature, too, just like it is in theirs. When you catch a glimpse of the divine in another person's performance, it is a reminder of what dwells in all of us, not just them. No one feels good all the time, no matter who they are, and the modern cult of happiness that pervades our society is misguided. We just don't work that way. That means, for those of us working on a skill hoping to improve it, we need to just keep going but not take it so seriously. Just play. As my friend and mentor Garret Kramer says, 'Stay in the game.' For goodness sake, Leonardo da Vinci is reported to have said that he thought he had offended God and mankind because (to him) his work 'didn't reach the quality it should have'. To me, if even the greatest genius in history felt insecure about his creative output, there's hope for all of us! So, when you see someone excelling, and it seems to you that they have some divine source of excellence, just remember – you're right – but so then do you.

Feedback, Jim, But Not As We Know It

So, if our thoughts and feelings aren't telling us about the outside world, about our circumstances, or about other people, for what reason should we listen to them at all? Well – there's a very important reason. They are telling us about our perspective, or lack thereof, in that moment. For that reason, they are a beautifully designed guidance system that never lies. We are always feeling our thinking, by which I mean the energy of THOUGHT. If we've gone outside-in, we can think of it as a warning light illuminating in our car. Instead of it warning us about problems in someone else's car, about intercontinental climate patterns, or about whether it's time for an upgrade; all it's doing is giving us feedback on how reliable the car (our worldview) is at that moment. If we aren't seeing clearly and our awareness is blinkered, it may not be the best time to evaluate our career progress. Also, just because we feel insecure, it may not be the time to hit the practice room or grind through another hour at the gym. It might not be the time to keep forcing new ideas for the next album. The more we see our feelings for what they really are – feedback on our thinking – the less sense it makes to judge them. The less it seems like a feeling is a problem, the less time we'll spend trying to solve it. It's all part of the ride. This is how true tenacity and resilience work, because once we see this, we find that there is no such thing as a *real* setback or a problem. The experience of a problem is just a warning light guiding us back to clarity.

Chapter 3 Summary

MYTHS about CONSCIOUSNESS

1. The human race is divided into various categories – talented, untalented, strong, weak, confident, shy, introvert, extrovert, etc

2. If you think someone seems superhuman that means they are.

3. Your sporting, musical or intellectual idols have the answers to how to be continually strong, confident or happy. You should sniff out all their secrets.

4. It is possible to have a good morning, a bad year, or a difficult life.

5. Each person, situation, circumstance, piece of music or other external trigger causes a corresponding internal response.

6. Some thoughts or feelings are bad, others are good. We must chase the good ones and avoid the bad ones.

7. Feelings are a guidance system telling us how the world is and what to do about it.

8. Whatever you think about yourself is true.

TRUTHS about CONSCIOUSNESS:

1. The capacity for effortless excellence is in every one of us.

2. Even if it appears that someone doesn't have natural mood swings, it isn't true.

3. Even your idols are human – just like you. Anyone who has ever lived has experienced psychological ups and downs. No exceptions.

4. Your experience is only ever created in the moment.

5. Emotions can appear to be caused by all sorts of external factors, but they are only ever created internally.

6. Ebb is not bad, and flow is not good. All emotions are harmless.

7. Our ups and downs only ever tell us about THOUGHT in the moment. Feelings *are* a guidance system but one that tells us how reliable our perspective is.

8. You are that which thinks, not the content of your thoughts.

FOUR

SUPERSTITION AIN'T THE WAY

There are basically two kinds of philosophy. One's called Prickles, the other's called Goo. And prickly people are precise, rigorous, logical. They like everything chopped up and clear. Goo people like it vague. For example, in physics, prickly people believe that the ultimate constituents of matter are particles. Goo people believe it's waves. And in philosophy, prickly people are logical positivists and goo people are idealists. And they're always arguing with each other, but what they don't realise is that neither one can take his position without the other person. Because you wouldn't know you advocated prickles unless there was somebody else advocating goo. You wouldn't know what a prickle was unless you knew what goo was. Because life is not either prickles or goo, it's gooey prickles and prickly goo.

Alan Watts, *The Nature of Consciousness*

These days we tend to be looking for prickly answers to our problems, but when we're talking about human

43

beings, we can't avoid the fact that goo is in their nature. It always has been. Psychologists were interested in the soul when the field was in its infancy, but as it gradually became pricklier and pricklier, somehow people stopped looking for goo at all. Whether you're more of a prickles person, or whether goo is more your thing, it's fair to say that all human beings intuitively know that a living creature is greater than the sum of its parts. We all sense an aliveness, but this 'life force' hasn't been terribly well represented by science, and perhaps this is an indicator that a rethink is in order.

Expert Performance And Psychology's Predicament

Science is highly valued in today's society and rightly so. On the backs of scientific breakthroughs, technological advances are connecting people, disseminating information, powering economies, curing disease and helping the human race to evolve and grow. But is it possible that in the spirit of advancing science, psychology's investigations into expert performance could have led us down a blind alley? It wouldn't be the first time that science had taken a wrong turn and needed to go back to the drawing board. Einstein liked thought experiments. So, let's give it a go...

WHEN SUPERSTITION MEETS TRUTH

- If a modern-day surgeon were able to speak with a colleague from the 1830s, he would hear all about clinical techniques that had seemed advanced for the time but had taken an incomplete paradigm as their basis. Although the 19th-century medic would have been steeped in the *latest* understanding, the modern surgeon would no doubt be struck by his colleague's basic *mis*understanding. Without an awareness of the role of germs, a key piece of the puzzle was missing.

• Equally, if a medieval stargazer were able to attend a lecture on the heliocentric (sun-centred) model of the solar system given by a modern astrophysicist, he would definitely be impressed by the accuracy of the modern calendar system that doesn't need to be adjusted periodically, but he would probably be outraged by the apparently heretical claim that the sun, rather than the earth, was at the centre. While it certainly looks like the sun rises and sets, even schoolchildren today know that the earth actually goes round the sun.

• Finally, if a modern-day flat-earther (they do exist) could sit down for a beer with a naval sea captain, there would be an argument. The skeptic would be mystified by how confidently his friend could speak of navigating around the earth, not once fearing that he would steer his crew off the edge, despite the flat-earther being vehemently convinced it works another way. Today, although most of us take for granted that the earth is round, some people live superstitiously because of a misunderstanding.

Each of these situations highlights the difference between harbouring a misunderstanding and simply knowing truth – not one's personal truth, but *the* truth. Historically speaking, when superstition and truth have collided, thus begins what is referred to as a 'paradigm shift'. Though the term has been abused somewhat, in the true sense, a paradigm shift is a major change to a prevailing scientific framework. The shift is so fundamental that it alters the experimental practices of the entire discipline.

PSYCHOLOGY'S PARADIGM SHIFT

Most people aren't aware that such a shift has actually already begun in psychology – something that has massive implications, not only for anyone wanting to master a skill or create specific results, but also for humankind, as we shall see.

Thomas Kuhn, who first coined the phrase, outlined the process by which paradigm shifts occur. Because we are talking about such a large-scale rethink and the truth reaching the collective consciousness, a paradigm shift is never an immediate process. It also never happens without considerable resistance at first. It took some 140 years for the idea that the earth orbits the sun to reach a more widespread acceptance. Until then, people had universally believed something that simply wasn't true. It took more than forty years for germ theory to be widely accepted, and though the ancient Greeks knew that the earth was round, it took

many hundreds of years for the idea of the flat earth
to (largely!) be laid to rest.

Figure 3.1: Phases of a paradigm shift

PHASE	CHARACTERISTICS
1. Pre-Paradigm	First, there are several incompatible and incomplete theories. Then, there is some consensus of opinion. Finally, a paradigm is established.
2. Normal Science	Investigations are framed by the dominant paradigm. But anomalies remain – facts that are difficult to explain within the context of the existing paradigm. Normal science becomes difficult as weaknesses in the old paradigm are revealed.
3. Crisis	The old paradigm is unable to explain anomalies, despite attempts.
4. Paradigm Shift	A scientific revolution – the old paradigm is rejected.
5. Post-Revolution	The new paradigm is established. Normal science resumes, solving puzzles from a more-complete understanding.

PERFORMANCE: THE ELEPHANTS IN THE ROOM

Several clues let us know that we are ripe for a psychological paradigm shift.

1. **Psychology lacks laws.**
Whereas the physical and natural sciences have well-established laws underpinning chemistry, biology, and physics, mainstream psychology, on the other hand, has yet to discover the principles behind all psychological experiences. In many ways, it still doesn't stand on 'solid ground', as William James put it.

2. **Complex and conflicting theories.**
In the absence of such laws, researchers are loath to rule anything out, resulting in numerous, conflicting theories and schools of thought. Some say nature, some say nurture. Some say it's about talent, others say it's purely about putting the time in. Others say it's not about putting in time, it's about quality of practice. Though there are similarities, top performers seem to report a variety of different practices. What psychology doesn't have is real explanation or consensus.

3. **Approaches that are widely accepted generate anomalous outcomes.**
The standard mental performance 'tools' don't get predictable results. Breathing techniques don't always calm us down, visualisations don't always inspire us or manifest the results they claim to be able to, mindfulness or meditation don't always make us more present. Applying a strict practice regime gets varying results. Willpower and grit

aren't predictors for the most successful careers. If these methods were grounded in truth or principles they would produce reliable, predictable results. They do not, so something else must be at play underneath the surface.

4. **Correlation is disguised as causation.**
As a result of not understanding what causes psychological experiences, many so-called experts essentially stab in the dark and investigate trends among the outcomes. These then get reported as causes, often by the media, and while there may be a grain of truth in some of them, true causation is not known. We hear reports that suggest a cause has been proven when in fact it has not been. How many times do we hear something like 'a new study *suggests* a link between X and the flow state', or 'researchers at The University of Somewhere believe that visualisation techniques can cause Y'. These kinds of statements make for good reading, but how much truth has actually been uncovered and how much confusion still remains?

Depending on how you look at it, the field of psychology currently finds itself in one of Kuhn's first two phases – with many muddled theories and without a single paradigm that accounts for the anomalies. That situation is changing, however.

The Inside-Out Revolution

The paradigm shift began in an unlikely place, with a Scottish welder living off the coast of Canada. A gentleman called Sydney Banks had a series of insights that were to turn our understanding of the mind inside-out. Although some of the ideas that Banks uncovered had been known in various forms for centuries, bringing them together as one set of psychological principles had never been done before. Banks's work has already filtered through into many arenas: mental health, sport, education, business, coaching, and, more recently, the performing arts. But it has not yet reached the collective consciousness in the same way that something like the round earth has. Importantly, there is an embryonic but growing body of research into the success of the principle-based approach.[2]

As you'll notice, I've already begun explaining how the new paradigm plays out for us performers, but in this chapter we'll look at the whole thing in a nutshell in order to illustrate just how far-reaching the implications are.

How It Really Works

1. THOUGHT is a spiritual energy – something far greater than we've realised. It's more than just ideas, calculations, brain activity, concepts or opinions. It is the creative energy that generates all things.

---

2. For more information visit www.3pgc.org/research

2. We don't just think thoughts *about* things, we 'think' our whole perception of the world and all our feelings. Our experience of everything we see, hear, feel, smell, and taste is processed through THOUGHT and is being *projected* by us rather than being data-*received*. Reality is all one divine illusion.

3. Each thought, feeling or perception is simultaneously created and experienced. Our perceptual experience only ever works from the inside-out.

4. THOUGHT has an energy of its own – it cannot be controlled by the intellect because the intellect is a creation. It isn't what is doing the creating.

5. The word THOUGHT, when used to denote the principle, is synonymous with the word 'spirit' – (universal) MIND – whatever you call the life energy that makes your heart beat. This is the *capacity* for, not the contents of your personal thoughts. What THOUGHT 'is' is the same as what CONSCIOUSNESS 'is'. They are all one spiritual energy.

6. We are able to *notice* that THOUGHT is generating reality – that is to say, we are aware that we think. The 'meaning' of our thoughts, feelings and perceptions only exists in CONSCIOUSNESS and is changeable like the weather.

7. Contained in the words THOUGHT, CONSCIOUSNESS and MIND is actually a THOUGHT-feeling-spirit connection. The new paradigm is that these three are actually all one and the same psycho-

spiritual energy. This stands independently of religion, belief, or circumstance; it is impersonal – it is a psychological, spiritual fact.

What most people are referring to when they use the word 'thought' is only a fraction of the true nature of what's actually at play – it's not the whole thing and it works a different way. The word THOUGHT is actually like a Russian nesting doll that contains many dolls within – it's almost like several of our old words overlap in a way we never realised. THOUGHT overlaps with 'feeling' and 'spirit', whereas we used to think they were distinct things. Separating them was only an idea, not a truth. As I said, elements of this understanding are not new; what's new is the fact that they are all one.

The principle of THOUGHT: The creative mechanism by which 100% of our thoughts, feelings and perceptions of reality are generated, moment-to-moment.

The principle of CONSCIOUSNESS: The fact of awareness – and that THOUGHT ebbs and flows within this awareness. This is the true cause of any emotional state. We started exploring this in Chapter 3.

The principle of MIND: The fact that we are alive. All things are part of this same energy. This aliveness is the very nature of THOUGHT and CONSCIOUSNESS, and this energy is all one. It's the way that all information naturally flows in the universe – how a heart knows how to beat, how a bud knows how to open. It's the power source behind our personal thoughts, our awareness and behind all life. We can't say it's something that the intellect is in charge of, because MIND also creates the intellect.

'What Has This Got To Do With Musical Excellence?'

I thought you might ask that. Because these are the underlying facts of how all human experiences work, these three principles underpin everything. Absolutely everything. Understanding this explains the cause of a whole host of otherwise seemingly disconnected phenomena: mental illness, conflict, violence, racism, inequality, war, substance abuse, personality, community, poverty, discrimination, learning, inspiration, leadership, and excellence. Our purpose here though is to focus specifically on musical excellence. The next few chapters are all about how deepening your understanding of these simple principles can be transformative in many areas, including mastering a skill or an art form. Much like other paradigm shifts, it is the new perspective, in and of itself, that is transformative. For example, once you understand that germs cause disease, you don't need to practise knowing it – you just live with a new understanding and new actions, like hand washing, come about from there. This is how this book can help you.

Seeing Through The Outside-In Illusion Brings You Closer To Truth

Although the truth is that our feelings can never be caused by anything on the outside, and THOUGHT creates 100% of our moment-to-moment felt experience, we live in a world that, on the whole, has yet to discover this for itself. Coupled with that, we each have areas where we see this simple truth more clearly than others. I guarantee that in some areas of your life it will already be easy for you to see that your feelings are internally generated. In other areas, I also guarantee that there will be times when you act as if a circumstance, situation, person, the weather – you name it – is causing your feelings. I can guarantee it because of these principles. The ebb and flow of THOUGHT within CONSCIOUSNESS means we cannot experience the truth all the time. We can *know* it though. This is why understanding is key, because even when we're experiencing the illusion of an outside-in world (and we all have to), if we understand the principles, we'll insightfully see through the illusion and remember the Inside-Out truth. It's the same confidence we have that germs are there, even though we don't experience them with the naked eye. Understanding trumps a convincing illusion.

As soon as we begin to see the truth that 100% of our feelings are THOUGHT-generated, our old superstitious actions stop making sense to us. Most obviously this involves all kinds of looking 'outside' ourselves for answers – including depending on any kind of 'success formula'. This is the outside-in misunderstanding. And it is why I said you wouldn't really find 'how-to's in this book. Many musicians, for example, practise in order to try and feel a certain way – confident, happy, fulfilled, or whatever – but, as we've seen, feelings just don't work that way. Because feelings are created on the inside, it's not actually possible for feelings to come from anything other than the principle of THOUGHT taking form in the moment. THOUGHT and feeling cannot be separated.

Figure 3.2: Truth vs. superstition

UNDERSTANDING (TRUTH)	MISUNDERSTANDING (SUPERSTITION)
Knowing the Inside-Out fact	*Tricked by the outside-in illusion*
Insightfully knowing that all psychological experience works from the inside-out.	Falsely attributing certain feelings or experiences to external factors.
Knowing we can only ever feel THOUGHT in the moment, even though feelings can seem to come from elsewhere.	Experiencing a circumstance, a situation, another person's actions, etc, as a problem, without realising what actually creates problems.

UNDERSTANDING (TRUTH)	MISUNDERSTANDING (SUPERSTITION)
Insightfully remembering what we really are – pure awareness.	Believing we are a separate body, personality, entity.
Having a human experience.	Fighting the human experience.
Having a wide range of emotions without experiencing them as a problem.	Avoiding, being confused by, and/or being afraid of certain emotions.
Looking in the right direction (inwards) for answers.	Looking in the wrong direction (outwards) for answers.
Psychologically effortless.	Psychological resistance.

Other examples of superstitious behaviour might include:

- Practising to avoid embarrassment or guilt.
- Not sharing something you have created so that you can avoid feeling criticised.
- Always asking a teacher to 'fix' your problems.
- Taking drugs (of any kind) to be more creative, energised or relaxed.
- Using mental techniques to try and guarantee a particular feeling.

- Struggling financially because you (subconsciously) believe that suffering causes you to feel inspired and create good art.

- Copying someone's mannerisms, phrases, or ways of dressing to feel like a star.

- Copying someone's practice or warm-up routines unquestioningly in order to emulate their results.

- Measuring progress by the amount of hours you put in.

- Constantly searching for new equipment (be it mouthpieces, strings, pedals or gadgets) to up your game.

- Pursuing achievements in order to feel a certain way about yourself.

- Keeping your diary relatively empty in order to avoid feeling overwhelmed.

These and all other superstitious actions have their roots in the outside-in misunderstanding. That's not to say that going outside-in is wrong, because it isn't. But the message in this chapter is that it's useful to know what's really going on. As the outside-in misunderstanding goes against the grain psychologically, it generates extra thinking that clouds our heads and takes an immense amount of energy to maintain. This misunderstanding complicates our thinking whereas the Inside-Out understanding simplifies it. As superstition gradually melts away, so, too, do all superfluous steps in our creative process, and we find ourselves experiencing less and less resistance. This is why exploring the Inside-Out understanding ('looking inward', or examining the nature of THOUGHT) is the single most leveraging action we can take as an artist. It's the creative equivalent of removing noise from a broadcast signal by tuning in more precisely to the source.

To quote Stevie Wonder, 'When we believe in things that we don't understand, then we suffer'. Each time a little piece of misunderstanding is removed, and we become more aligned with how things really work, our understanding takes an expansive leap and our background suffering recedes. As we saw in Chapter 3, our awareness will always ebb and flow, but understanding is more about what we know to be true. We can *know* it, without *seeing* it fully at a particular moment. To continue the germ analogy, no matter what mood you are in, it is always a good idea to wash your hands after going to the toilet, because of the truth of *how the system works*. This is about clarity of understanding. Our understanding of the principles deepens in increments – insights – and as we see more clearly, we no longer see the world quite as it was before. Superstition of any kind will block us on the path to whatever it is we are trying to achieve. Deepening our understanding, on the other hand, will always reacquaint us with the limitless potential that is our nature.

Stripping away superstitious thinking helps us to see the wood for the trees, namely that your feelings are always telling you about the shape that THOUGHT is taking in the moment. Is a big gig making you anxious? Actually, that'll be anxious thinking causing that. Frustrated by a situation? No, that'll be the frustrated thinking you aren't noticing. Feel inspired from a good motivational speech? Actually, there's no such thing – it's all an inside job. All THOUGHT. I hope by now that you are starting to see that this paradigm isn't something you can really *apply* as such, because it's merely just a pointer to something that is true whether you try and do anything about it or not. But over the next few chapters, I'll be explaining some of the ways that it specifically plays out as we master a skill. Chapter 5 is about learning and practice, and Chapter 6 is about treading a longer-term path towards mastery. Getting more deeply in touch with your innate source of excellence is a subtractive process, as I have said, so continue with an open mind and let's see how much superstition we can lose...

Chapter 4 Summary

MYTHS about superstition

1. People are entitled to believe what they want to, so all beliefs are valid.

2. Superstitions tend to be small and insignificant things such as: thinking black cats bring bad luck, avoiding walking under ladders, knocking on wood.

3. Giving over to superstition is quirky, harmless fun.

4. 'Truth' has a fundamentalist, religious overtone to it. One person's truth is another person's lie.

5. Changing our habits is difficult; it takes a long time and is an additive process.

6. There is no superstition in modern science.

TRUTHS about superstition

1. People do indeed have the freedom to believe what they want, but we can't avoid the fact that there are underpinning principles behind how various domains function. Such domains include physics, chemistry, biology, and psychology.

2. Believing the outside-in illusion is the most common superstition, and it can have huge implications in every area of your life.

3. When we are unaware of the principles behind human experience, superstition can complicate simple processes and can cause confusion and suffering.

4. Truth is simply a matter of facts. It's not a matter of loyalty, personality, or dogma. Universal principles don't need to be believed in. They just quietly exist whether they are understood or not. Learning about the way the human experience works saves considerable energy, but it's not compulsory.

5. Change is only ever spontaneous. Each time we have an insight, we understand the truth more deeply, and superstition suddenly becomes obsolete. This affects our actions by implication. This is always a subtractive process.

6. A paradigm shift occurs when a significant misunderstanding that has been the basis for a scientific field is resolved. Misunderstanding and superstition are essentially the same thing.

FIVE

SOMETHING INSIDE SO STRONG

There is an old Chinese fable about a rice farmer. He was very ambitious for his crop to grow tall and strong, and he wanted to do everything he could to help. Soon after setting the seed, he checked the soil for signs of life. Finally, after several days of agonising wait, he noticed as the seedlings began to quietly break through the surface of the soil. As he continued to monitor their growth for several days, he became more and more impatient. Desperately wanting his crop to grow tall and strong just like his friends' crops, he eventually came up with an ingenious plan. Every day, one by one, he gently encouraged the seedlings to grow faster by pulling on the leaves. Painstakingly, he tended to each plant in the same way and laboured for many hours every day, harder than any of his friends were working. Sure enough, for the first couple of days the seedlings started to sit a little higher and look a little taller. But gradually, by the third day, he noticed that his beloved plants were withering and dying – within a week, only the few seedlings that had accidently been left untouched grew tall and strong.

The farmer in this ancient story had the best intentions. He had seen other farmers' successful rice crops and wanted to emulate them, so he laboured and toiled away to try and guarantee the outcome he had set his heart on. But in spite of his solid work ethic, he missed one crucial truth that eventually became his stumbling block: that the seedlings did not need his intervention. Provided that their basic needs were met, the seedlings themselves would take care of the rest. Growing tall and strong was already in their nature, and not only were the farmer's efforts wasted, they actually stifled the young plants. Just as an acorn has 'tree-ness' within it, the rice seedlings had a natural intelligence already animating them, from the inside-out. This intelligence is the principle of (Universal) MIND – the fact that, just like us, the plants are alive and with that aliveness comes an innate source of universal wisdom, a wisdom that knows how to overcome, to grow, and to flourish. Mother Nature has a MIND of her own, and if left to run her course, will produce excellent rice crops, although, admittedly, 'excellence' is probably the last thing the seedlings would be concerned with. MIND is incredibly sophisticated, too – plants 'know' how to arrange their leaves and follow the sun, extract nutri-

ents from the soil, and develop spontaneously in a way
that is context sensitive. They instinctively know when
it is time to flower, lie dormant, or go to seed. If their
roots start growing into a rock, they have the intelligence to grow around. If a plant is damaged, it somehow heals itself. Because the farmer underestimated
the innate potential his crops possessed (by virtue of
the fact they were alive), he ended up with a fraction
of the harvest he could have had. So, too, is the case
with our musical practice – we often underestimate the
innate wisdom that has been supporting us all along.

When you stop and think about it, plants are very
wise and so are you. Call this 'excellence' if you like,
although I'm not sure a plant would care that much.
Universal MIND, wisdom, Mother Nature, 'God', or
life, are all names for that which powers our little seedlings' moments of genius. If your hackles have gone
up because I dropped the G-bomb, then I apologise,
but when we shelve any kind of religious overtone,
what we are really left with is nature's innate gift for
spontaneously doing whatever needs to be done in the
moment, so that life flourishes. I'm not talking here
about God as a separate entity. This is the 'God'-ness
within.

How To Avoid MIND-less Practice

Let me be clear – the intelligence of universal MIND
is always at play. It's part of nature. It's the rhythm of

life. But we musicians can sometimes neglect the fact that we are part of this creative wisdom and instead try to micromanage our music just as the farmer did with his poor seedlings. Whenever we do this, our attention is diverted – we focus on outcome, we over-think, and we relinquish our creative gifts. The (finite personal) mind may strive and plan, but inspired action only ever happens in the now. In our practice, what fuels our spontaneous musical choices is insight – fresh thought coming from within, born of the living moment. It never comes from the outside, it comes from (universal) MIND – spiritual energy – and this energy has a tendency to create flow on its own. In other words, from an uncluttered headspace, free of superstitious thinking, we are more open to the inner cues that let us know precisely which actions need to be taken in any given moment. This is important, if we think about it, because artistic growth spurts tend to happen when we follow our nose and go with our intuition. This may sound like I'm talking about abandoning discipline altogether, but in fact it's the exact opposite. 'Disciplined' practice has little to do with rigidly following a prescription, and much more to do with taking the action that the present moment requires, regardless of whether it feels good. We intui-tively know what's required, whether that be listening, taking a break, reading, having a lesson, drilling an exercise, or putting in more hours. The moment that we start to 'pull at the leaves', or get tricked by the outside-in illusion, is when we mistake these *effects* of inspiration for the cause. Top performers (and therefore many of your teachers and idols) are notoriously bad at explaining what caused their success. Instead, what they'll usually do is describe what they noticed and then put it down to that. This is the same correlation/causation issue I mentioned in Chapter 1, and it can trick us into blindly following advice on the premise that someone 'out there' has all the answers. They don't. What drives your 'deliberate practice' is Mother Nature, not your intellect or your idol's. It is the universal MIND, not our finite mind that guides how our craft unfolds. Given that it all takes place in a constant flow of awareness, it would be a mistake to think that an insight that prompted great results in one moment could be re-applied or transplanted indiscriminately. This is precisely what happens when a golfer tries to follow Tiger Woods's training regime, or we superstitiously stick to the same rituals that got us our big break, or conversely, when we are trying too hard to be original.

1. Just play.

Your whole practice experience is THOUGHT-generated; yet, included in this creation is a whole set of beliefs that may appear to be objectively true but are actually subjective:

- How 'difficult' (unfamiliar) or 'easy' (familiar) something seems.

- How well or badly you think you are doing.

- Whether you think you're working hard enough.

- Whether you feel like you're learning.

- Whether something seems like a priority to work on.

- Whether you feel you need a teacher or coach's input.

- Whether you think you've improved.

- All comparisons between where you think you are and where you think you should be.

- Whether you feel 'like practising'.

Understanding is everything. The simple truth is that THOUGHT creates reality, but it does such a good job that it can convince us it didn't do it. As you realise that *all* psychological experiences (thoughts, feelings, perceptions) are created from the inside-out, but that life will often appear to be working outside-in, you experience increasing creative and emotional freedom. It will liberate your music making and open your mind and body, because it will let you in on the cosmic joke – that we can think and feel things that aren't true. Sometimes we believe our thoughts. Seeing this will remind you that even the most 'personal' problems are created impersonally via THOUGHT, so there is no feeling we need avoid and no feeling to pursue. Psychological resistance is optional, so you can go with the flow and just play without overthinking.

2. Don't navigate by what feels good. Navigate by *what is true.*

Anyone who has ever played a musical instrument to a reasonable standard will have had the experience of practising something they knew needed doing, even though they didn't feel like doing so at the time. They practise what they intuitively know they need to instead of following the voices in their head ('I don't want to', 'I can't', 'I'm hungry', etc) because they understand something fundamental about the mind, that their thoughts can seem to be telling them one thing, yet they can take action motivated by something deeper. This is because whilst there is always an innate urge to learn and develop ('I want to master my arpeggios', or 'I want to have a more beautiful tone'), there is also a more transient kind of thought that pops up ('I don't enjoy arpeggios', 'I find working on fundamentals boring'). We usually stumble across this fact of how the mind works early on in our musical journey. And while it may seem very obvious, I mention it here because we can easily see it in one context but miss that it actually applies to 100% of our experience. Making decisions based on what feels good and avoiding what feels bad is a lousy way of navigating

life, even on the occasions you don't notice yourself
doing it. (And we all have them!)

The thing is, we need to understand what practice
is and what it *isn't*. Even though we can feel confident
when we've practised, practice isn't there to *make* us
feel confident. There will be times when we will feel
nervous even though we have prepared thoroughly.
Equally, we can't put in the hours and thereby effectively avoid embarrassment – feelings are created by
THOUGHT, not by skill. There are other implications
to this. It also means that just because we had a particularly good practice session, it doesn't mean we will
feel the same feeling each time we play that same piece.
This is a very common misunderstanding – that some
feelings are right and others are wrong. For a long time,
I believed that some kind of feeling of struggle was
necessary in order for me to have put in proper 'hard
work', which just isn't true. Effective practice is more
about simply showing up and being open-minded
enough to conduct musical experiments. From there,
we can let the wisdom of the moment carry us away.
Navigate from a place of understanding rather than a
place of superstition.

3. Look inward, and the 'how-to's will follow.

There is definitely a place for following an instruction
method, exploring what has worked for other people,
planning your practice routine and having life goals,
but if you want to do something other than 'pull on

the leaves' of your music, an understanding of how THOUGHT actually works is indispensable. When I say 'look inward', I'm not trying to be esoteric. I'm also not instructing you to sit in a cave and meditate before you make music, although you can if you want to. I'm simply pointing you back to the wisdom of the true self – look to the moment for the answers you seek. Listen for what comes to you in the now. Feel for what strikes you. Notice what occurs internally, and then act accordingly.

The following questions may be helpful:

- How does my body, my breathing, my instrument feel right now?

- Who (or perhaps what) is experiencing that body, that breathing, that instrument?

- What thoughts, ideas and emotions are coming up right here, right now?

- Where do I think those feelings are coming from?

- Do they seem to be created from the outside-in (happening to a separate self) or from the inside-out (from the true self)?

- As I sit here now, what do I want?

- If I didn't have to avoid or chase a feeling, what would I do?

- What makes sense to me to do in this moment?

Again, these questions are not meant as another ritual or practice to be followed, and they certainly aren't the prescription for spiritual enlightenment. Consider the ones that make sense, discard the ones that don't. It's your call. Progress in your craft only ever occurs via insight. It can't come from new equipment, banishing negative thoughts, visualising success, deep breathing, following an expert's regime, or any other leaf-pulling attempts to force change. Those are just ways of managing symptoms, not dealing with causes. Insight leads, and action follows spontaneously.

4. Let go of the idea that there is a right way to practise.

Maybe you were told that practice should always sound good. Or perhaps you have a trusty warm-up routine that you always use. I used to have a long list of things that I felt weren't allowed in my practice – like making mistakes without correcting them, or starting to play without thinking about my posture. Again, I'm not telling what you should or shouldn't do. Instead, I'm gently inviting you to consider that some aspects of your music making may be a little more rigid than they could be. That's no bad thing, but it's helpful to realise when we are superstitiously clinging to ideas of right and wrong, instead of noticing what the moment requires. The only way that should concern you is *your* way, here and now. The formless principle of THOUGHT takes form *in the moment*, so there's an inherent spontaneity about our decision-making, musical practice and creativity. Someone once asked the innovative French composer Claude Debussy what rules he followed when he was writing music, and he famously replied, *mon plaisir*, or 'my pleasure'. What a seedling needs to do one day is not necessarily what it needs to do the next. Listen for the inner cues, arising in the moment, and act accordingly.

5. Don't try to override wisdom with the perfect plan. Do what you know is right in the moment.

You have an innate ability to get lost in your practice and go about it with a light-hearted openness. It's called 'play' for a reason, after all. I've known many musicians to stick to a very rigid practice routine even when it's obvious to them they should deviate from it. I knew a wind player who religiously stuck to his three-hour practice plan even when he had a chest infection, because he thought breaking his regime would mean he wasn't serious! Breaking or changing your routine isn't necessarily about lacking discipline – you might be ready for a change or a rest. Also, to do something just because you fancy trying it out is a valid reason. In fact, don't forget that you are allowed to have fun! Just as the seedling is guided by Mother Nature's wisdom, MIND is steering your progress. Have the confidence to listen for what MIND is telling you and be prepared to be shown the way.

Figure 5.1: Practice from the Inside-Out vs. outside-in

(INSIDE-OUT) INSIGHTFUL PRACTICE.	(OUTSIDE-IN) LEAF PULLING.
Following inner cues.	Following outer cues.
Openness.	Closed-mindedness.
Responding to the moment.	Responding to superstitious thinking.
Focus is a result.	Focus is a tactic.
A course of action flows spontaneously from fresh thinking and is always subject to change.	The moment is ignored in favour of a stale, fixed idea about what is 'proper' practice.
Knowing your job is to get out of the way and let nature take its course.	Forcing change by getting in the way and trying to do nature's job.
The musician is ready for insights.	The musician is only interested in results and ignores insight altogether.

Chapter 5 Summary

MYTHS about practice

1. Progress is directly caused by the amount of time spent practising, the number of repetitions performed, or by finding the perfect exercise or training method.

2. Feeling like you are working hard is important, so progress always requires sacrifice, struggle, willpower, or psychological effort.

3. It would be foolish not to follow an expert's advice about what and how to practise.

4. It is difficult to know if you are taking the right actions in your practice.

5. Your feelings tell you about how your practice is going.

6. Success in any field requires students to develop motivation, resilience, persistence, creativity, and to find their purpose.

7. Practise until you feel proud and confident. Practise until you don't experience embarrassment or guilt. Practise until you feel good enough. Boredom is a sign to stop.

8. Effortless, effective practice is something few can achieve.

TRUTHS about practice

1. Effective practice usually involves investing a lot of time, performing certain actions rather than others, and a great deal of repetition, but these are effects rather than the causes of an insightful learning process.

2. The root cause of musical progress (or any learning) is a fresh thought or a realisation – an insight.

3. Listening to experts' advice can be extremely helpful, but the buck stops with your own sense of what's right.

4. Unhindered by overthinking, right action occurs spontaneously.

5. Your feelings merely tell you about the condition of your thinking. This natural internal process lets you know how clear (or not!) your perspective is.

6. Motivation, resilience, persistence, creativity and purpose are all innate capacities. They cannot and need not be learnt or built. They are only ever uncovered.

7. Practise because you want to. No amount of practice can guarantee a particular feeling. All the practice in the world cannot stop certain feelings from happening, and practice cannot prove anything about you. Navigate by what is true, not by feelings.

8. Effortless, effective practice is a result of understanding and insight.

SIX

I CAN SEE CLEARLY
NOW THE RAIN
HAS GONE

*'If you end up with a boring miserable life because you
listened to your mom, your dad, your teacher, your priest,
or some guy on television telling you how to do your shit,
then you deserve it.'*

Frank Zappa

In August 2012, I was a single man. And although I
wasn't particularly searching for happiness, part of
me knew I wanted to find a partner. I was new to the
internet dating thing, but, flicking through the pictures,
one profile seemed intriguing. There was just one tiny
problem – the young woman that I assumed lived in
the UK was actually visiting from Moscow. She just
happened to be on holiday studying English and
was enjoying the buzz around the London Olympics.

Nevertheless, I sent the beautiful redhead a message, and we soon fixed a date. We met at St James's Park Tube station and then went for a tour around London, ending up at the Royal Festival Hall, where, fittingly, two years later, I would propose to her. Our first meeting was quickly followed up by another date the very next day, but the day after that she returned home. She had been in London for a month, but I had only discovered her during her last two days in the city.

We lived 1700 miles apart for two years, seeing each other only sporadically. The problem with a long-distance relationship, apart from the price of tickets, is that upon announcing that you are hopping on a plane again to Moscow to see your girlfriend, there will be no shortage of people giving you their opinions and advice. In retrospect, it sounds romantic; but at the time there was often a lot of justifying required, or so it seemed to the people asking the questions. What's going to happen in the future? Where are you both going to live? Won't you run out of money? Can't you find someone more local? All those fabulous questions and jokes about mail-order brides – hilarious. The interesting thing for me, looking back on that period now, was the sheer number of people with doubts and confusion about the vision, or who couldn't fathom what my future wife and I were doing. We, on the other hand, were confused by their lack of faith. My parents were polite and wise enough to say that they trusted me, yet I'm sure they must have at least discussed the possibility that I had totally lost my mind. But knowing what we now do about the principle of MIND, we know that losing 'my' mind is the one thing I hadn't done.

Like with all people who create, innovate, take a new direction, lead a movement, or in some way step out onto virgin territory, there was something pulling me. We can reflect on and even romanticise these bold, decisive moments in our lives, but that strong inner urge to be ourselves, even when we appear to be the only ones who know what that means, is an innate capacity. It can never be extinguished, it can only be obscured by errant thought. As our head clears, the essence of who we are is revealed again, and spontaneous, compelling and sometimes unexpected actions come as a result of that state of mind. All the while, though, it is only the creative spiritual energy of the principle of MIND that knows where our evolution will take us, not our intellect. The generative spiritual energy that saw Walt Disney bring Mickey Mouse and the entire Disney empire into being was the same energy that powered Steve Jobs's bold move from computers to music and then smartphones. The spirit of evolution and revolution that saw Madonna, Miles Davis or Stravinsky reinvent themselves countless times, was the same force of nature that had Gandhi liberate an entire nation from the rule of the British Empire. Again, it's absolutely *not* because these people were 'geniuses' that their innovative creations took form in the world – it was because of the innate predilection to evolve and grow that resides in every single one of us. This unity, rather than the illusion of separation, is the true heart of the matter. This is the nature of creativity, innovation and purpose.

Intuition: The Power Of The 'No-Brainer'

There seem to be two types of decision – the ones we think *we make* and the ones that seem to *be made on our behalf*. If I look back to when I started commuting a few thousand miles on a regular basis, in truth I don't ever remember making a decision. At no point did I weigh up the pros and cons of starting a long-distance relationship. I just found it happening because a sense of purpose overcame me, from a part of me far deeper than my intellect. This was an example, and we all have them, of instinctively knowing the right course of action and following our hunch *without a second thought*. It's only after the fact that these can seem like decisions we've made.

Throughout the period that Polina and I were travelling between London and Moscow there were plenty of occasions when we weren't clear-headed, or when one of us was seeing it and the other wasn't. But because we had been touched deeply enough by the insights that arose when we *were* seeing more clearly, and we had a deep enough understanding that it was only THOUGHT we were feeling, it never made sense to change course just because we experienced a doubtful feeling, or even just because we were sometimes down in the dumps. Leadership and innovation thrive on recognising the inability of a temporary feeling-state to thwart the accomplishment of the vision. Also, it is the secret to what really drives what psychologists call 'deliberate' practice. How do those rare musicians who change the face of their art form have the boldness and confidence to take a step onto virgin territory? How can we know when it is right to swim against the tide of popular opinion and when it isn't? What is the difference between misguided stubbornness and being a true visionary? How can we tell the difference between listening to wisdom and heading down a blind alley? Well, to tell the truth, it's a no-brainer. When you know, you know. Such no-brainers, a consequence of a clear head, nudge us back on course.

Not so long ago, Polina bought me a tandem parachute jump for my birthday – my first time doing this. During the training with a cool dude called Janos, I was very excited. I was keen to discover what it was like to jump out of a plane and plummet to the earth for a few minutes. I had spent a lot of mental energy imagining the jump itself and the initial few minutes in freefall, but a totally unexpected part of the experience for me was the beauty of the descent after the parachute had opened. As we gently floated down to earth there was a kind of blissful inevitability. We were being pulled by gravity but also supported by both the parachute and Janos's wisdom and experience. I could vaguely make out the airfield we were headed towards. I could see for miles and miles, but the interesting thing, as I dangled above the earth, was that I had so many options: I could look up at the parachute, I could look directly ahead at the sky in front of me, I could try in vain to see the whole support system behind me, I could close my eyes as I had when I jumped out of the plane, or I could just bear witness to the whole thing unfolding before me. *I* wasn't in charge – the principles of gravity and aerodynamics were. I was given the steering reins briefly to have a go at doing some spins, but it was obvious that if I got into difficulty then I would be nudged back on course. Once we landed, Janos told me that when the parachute had opened the ropes had twisted and, effectively, that he had saved my life. At the time, I knew he had had my back, though, and only when I think about it now do I realise how differently it could have turned out.

'MIND Has Your Back'

When my dear friend Dr John Countryman first said this to me, it blew me away. To imagine that I didn't have to micromanage my life was such a relief. If creative projects are anything like parachute jumps, we can very easily get tricked into thinking that's it's always our job to control the ride, almost as if it's necessary to somehow push the parachute every single millimeter of the way down to earth. Actually, the natural pull of gravity looks after that – it makes the whole journey not only possible but essentially effortless if we allow it to be. We can panic and cling on for dear life, we can relax and dangle, and we can sometimes nudge the parachute this way or that, but without the function of gravity there'd be no graceful descent. MIND provides the inevitable direction and support. It's always got 'your back,' as John told me.

Whenever we find ourselves jumping head first into the unknown or following a hunch without a second thought, then that's a clue into state of mind. An experience of flow is telling us about the clarity with which we see things at that particular moment. At these moments, it doesn't feel like we are making a decision to innovate, to go against the crowd, to hit 'pause' when we're told to press 'go' – it just seems to happen, because it makes sense. If we have to stop and weigh up whether we should follow a particular course of action, whether we're making a mistake, or whether we're being too bold, or too conservative, then that's not telling us about whether it's a good idea, about how dedicated we are, or about whether we're capable. That feeling is simply telling us about our thinking, because only THOUGHT creates our moment-to-moment experience.

Sometimes, the wisdom of MIND has us do seemingly strange things – taking a rest at a busy time, following a creative detour, gathering information before a bold move, becoming obsessed with something that may otherwise seem irrelevant. Just like gravity, the wisdom of MIND is not something we have to 'access' because it is always there naturally. We can't be separate from it. The true self *is* wisdom.

Hear me well here, because I'm definitely not saying to wait around for an inspired feeling until you take action. If you are searching for wisdom as another 'I'll be happy when', then you surely aren't following it. It's a bit like when Louis Armstrong was asked what jazz was, and he allegedly replied, 'Man, if you gotta ask, you're never gonna know.' Wisdom is your true essence, so if you feel like it's lacking, that can only mean you aren't noticing what's under your nose.

Figure 6.1: Innovation, from the Inside-Out

INSIDE-OUT (TRUTH)	OUTSIDE-IN (ILLUSION)
Invention, creativity and mastery are only driven by the innate, inner energy of MIND.	Acting under the illusion that knowledge, skill or ideas can be *put in* in some way.
The formless energy of THOUGHT crystalises as our ideas and experience of reality created in the moment.	From a clouded viewpoint, it looks like we are reliant on something or someone else for inspiration or wise counsel.

Purpose Is A Soul Thing, Not A Goal Thing

So what gets in the way of us following this innate wisdom in our practice, in our art, or in life? Well, it all comes back to the outside-in misunderstanding. Our entire experience works from the inside-out – not inside the body, not inside the brain, but deeper inside. From within the principle of MIND. Every one of us, at this shared core, is the same spiritual energy that is so beautiful, so resilient, and so creative that the only thing that can possibly stand in the way is when we misunderstand the inner cues and get tricked into believing the outside-in lie. Just as Frank Zappa says in the quote at the beginning of the chapter, if we mistakenly believe that someone else has a deeper source of wisdom than we do, we are then using this same innate, infinitely creative resource to justify why they are right and we are wrong. Maybe this is the advice to stay in music college, which for some might match their inner wisdom, but for others might not. Only we really know what is best for us. Staying on at Juilliard, for example, was right for Itzhak Perlman, but wrong for Miles Davis. There can't be a blanket policy, because wisdom is always context-sensitive, giving us whatever we need in the moment. Miles knew it was right *for him* to drop out, so he did. Often, when successful musicians who have followed their wisdom try to impart advice, they mistakenly put their success down to the action they took rather than to the fact that they followed their instinct. This is how we get stuck in practice rituals, warm-up techniques, or study methods designed for a different context.

The same is true for goal setting. Purpose and

motivation never actually come from setting a goal, only ever from an insight. By choosing behaviour over wisdom, we put the cart before the horse. The moment a goal is set, we can easily narrow our perceptual field to achieving it rather than remaining open to the subtle new options that arise out of every single moment. If we take action because it makes sense to us, then we stay on track. The moment we renounce our inner guidance system, the more quickly we can be led down a blind alley by someone else's advice. Follow the advice, set the goal if it makes sense to, but don't make the mistake of believing that received wisdom, or goals have any power in them – they don't. Let gravity itself do the hard work when you skydive!

Wisdom: How To Follow The Inner Voice

1. **Wisdom is always there, but look in the right direction.**

   As you continue to explore the Inside-Out nature of life, you'll begin to notice that no amount of looking outside yourself will ever tell you which direction your creative output should take, how you should structure your practice today, what best to invest your time in, how to build your career, or where to find your next innovative idea. The only place that kind of wisdom comes from is 'within' – the formless energy that creates. Look there. Look within.

2. **Remember – you are your only true teacher**
'You can lead a horse to water, but you can't make it drink', so the saying goes. The simple truth is that your teachers, idols, gurus or advisers cannot ever *give* you the answer you are searching for – it can only ever be pointed to. Don't try to follow someone else's plan slavishly, because ultimately it can't work. Take the parts that make sense to you and discard the rest. Trust the intelligence that creates your experience. Ultimately, it is *your* opinion that matters.

3. **There are no rules for how to be you**
If you buy into the idea that there are firm rules for how you should master your craft, develop your career, or live your life, then you are turning your back on the tailor-made insights you can have, crafted lovingly by MIND. Teachers and coaches teach their ideas as 'rules' when they mistakenly believe that an action (rather than an insight) can cause inner changes. There is no right way – only *your* way.

4. **Do or do not do. There is no 'try'.**
Creativity, innovation, leadership, and purpose are innate. When contaminated, superstitious, out-side-in thinking clears, what is left behind is the true self – among whose qualities is an unshakeable inner sense of direction. You are your own north star. Sometimes musicians tell me they are search-

ing for their 'sound' or their 'voice', but it's always already there – just say what you know needs to be said. Trying to be bold or original can be the death of creative leadership. THOUGHT is creative by its very nature, and the intelligence of MIND powers your unique gift to the world. I can assure you there is no need to try to be you.

5. **Fear of criticism is THOUGHT, too.**
   Ever hear that cheesy advice that fear is actually an acronym for **False Evidence Appearing Real?** Well, much as it gripes me to say it, there's a grain of truth in that, because *everything* THOUGHT generates appears real – that's just how THOUGHT rolls. But just because the evidence *appears* real, it doesn't necessarily mean you should alter your course of action. A fearful feeling is telling you about fearful thinking in the moment. Nothing else. If you know it's right for you in the moment, do it anyway.

6. **The right kind of action**
   Many famous coaches and teachers advocate taking massive action to get massive results, which can be effective – however, only if the actions you're taking are insightful. In other words, our massive, inspired actions in the world of *form* all stem from the *formless* inner world of THOUGHT energy. From infinite possibility to decision – a creation in the moment. If you take massive action merely because

someone says you must, then you aren't trusting insight, you're relying on a technique, which is the definition of outside-in. As a result, you just create busywork and head more quickly in the wrong direction. While you can't really ever do so, when your actions seem to bypass insight, all you do is jam up your head with extra thinking. Take massive action when insight moves you, sure, but more importantly, also take massive action when you intuitively know it is right but don't feel like doing it. This is how insight causes 'self-discipline' – we remember what we want, no matter what mood we're in.

Bill Evans is one my favourite jazz pianists. He had a lyrical, sophisticated style with a rich harmonic palette and an ingenious ability to weave an unexpected improvisation in the moment. He didn't see himself as particularly talented, though he was a monolithic influence on future musicians. In a 1966 documentary, *The Universal Mind of Bill Evans*, the great pianist explored the creative process and self-teaching. Amid the black-and-white charm, clouded by cigarette smoke, he gently challenges the outside-in assumption of the interviewer – his brother, Harry – about finding a musical voice and following a deeper spiritual purpose – what he refers to as the 'universal musical mind':

Harry: 'Don't we need someone to *feed in* procedures, and approaches, and tools, and mechanics of doing things – then we can depart?'

Bill: "Well I needed that, too, Harry, but the only thing is that *you* as an individual always make the decision about what you accept and what you reject... that's the thing that you as an artist are really concerned with."

You are on a learning journey, but it only ever works inside-out – even when it looks like it doesn't. Bill knew it and so do you.

Chapter 6 Summary

MYTHS about innovation, purpose and creativity

1. You either 'have it', or you don't.

2. You need external forces to motivate or inspire you to create something worthwhile.

3. You need to find your creative voice or life purpose.

4. Greatness is only achieved by knowing your outcome and setting goals.

5. There is a secret formula for excellence that needs to be learned.

TRUTHS about innovation, purpose, and creativity

1. Not only do you 'have it', you *are* it. You are the intelligent, formless, spiritual energy behind life.

2. Inspiration and motivation are only ever an inside job. Literally, *inspiration* means 'in the spirit'. And *courage* is 'heart strength'. The very fact that you are alive means you have them in abundance.

3. It's impossible to lose your creative voice or sense of purpose. You may lose sight of them from time to time, but they are always there.

4. Greatness is a by-product of insight. The capacity for greatness and the ability to have insights are innate.

5. The formula is innate, so it's no secret to you: insights, produced by MIND, nudge your work in the right direction. Follow your creative hunches and see where they lead.

SEVEN

I KNOW A MAN AIN'T SUPPOSED TO CRY

In my late teens and throughout my twenties, I suffered from debilitating shoulder pain whenever I played the violin. What began as a bit of soreness when I played quickly deteriorated into an overuse condition. By the time I was a performance major, I could barely play for more than twenty minutes at a time. Most of my days as a music undergraduate revolved around trying to manage a pain-rest-pain cycle. I tried everything I possibly could – painkillers, heat, ice, visits to doctors, trigger-point therapy, acupuncture, yoga, the Alexander Technique, more doctors, different violin equipment, physiotherapy – all to try and alleviate the pain. But the quest wasn't just physical. Increasingly, it became about alleviating emotional pain, too. The pain seemed to be proof that I was a musical failure, because I couldn't do the one thing I literally ached to do – to play, and to be loved for doing it. To me at that time, a musician who didn't play wasn't a proper musician, and, by implication, every twinge of pain meant *I* wasn't good enough. So, you see, because of my belief about the pain, I thought that for my own wellbeing I needed to stop those feelings at all costs.

To say my quest to 'solve' the shoulder pain was an obsession is an understatement. I kept detailed diaries of my experiments and meticulously notated every tiny alteration I made to the positioning of the violin chin rest and shoulder rest. I also tried literally hundreds of combinations of various shapes, sizes and materials. I even attempted, without success, to design my own violin fittings. Obsessively, I watched videos of other violinists for clues to what they were doing to be pain free. In addition, I adapted many of my daily activities in order not to feel bad: I avoided lying on my left-hand side when I went to sleep, and I chose clothes I thought wouldn't interfere with my shoulder when playing. This is to say nothing of the lengthy stretching and heating rituals I had created for myself. Increasingly, my life was revolving around my shoulder problem. Without noticing, although it appeared to be the only option, I had become stuck in the habit of searching 'outside' myself to change how I was feeling. Also, I was measuring my progress by how much pain I was noticing. After years of seeking, one concert performance revealed that I had been pointing my search in the wrong direction.

One summer, I went to hear the great Russian violinist Maxim Vengerov at the Royal Albert Hall. Vengerov is a megastar among violinists, and when I found out he was playing Lalo's *Symphonie Espagnol* in London, I was desperate to see him. This piece is a demanding violin concerto that explodes into action almost from the very moment it begins. In many ways, I was delighted to hear one of my musical heroes play live, but I especially remember taking this concert as an opportunity to study him. I watched him intensely to see how he was managing to be so successful. I imagined stepping into his shoes and wondering what it would feel like to be standing there as the soloist. Then the insecurities came: 'I will never play like that'; 'It's easy for him – he's got a Stradivari'; 'He's just a gifted alien from another planet that I'll never match'; 'I should give up playing the violin'. As he continued playing, I stood there watching the dazzling show of musicianship and virtuosity, and I noticed two things happen. First, I felt increasingly bad about myself – jealous of the great violinist's physical freedom and insecure about my own playing compared to his. At the time, it seemed he was causing my insecure feelings, and I never stopped to consider how absurd that really was. I became angry. Second, as the anger subsided, I became curious about why as I watched the concert my left shoulder was hurting more and more – in fact, it hurt as much as if I, myself, had been playing the violin all day. This confused me, because it was the summer break, and I had suspended my violin practice in order to give my shoulder a chance to recover. So, it couldn't have been violin practice causing pain at that moment, there couldn't have been a change in my shoulder muscles within the course of the concert, and there was no way that the concert itself could have caused the sudden change in pain. It had to be the mind alone. Was this even possible?

This was first time that I even contemplated looking inwards and bypassing the body in order to resolve the pain. Eventually, this insight would lead me to exploring the immense creative power of Thought and exactly how much of our moment-to-moment experience is Thought-generated – namely, all of it.

We've seen previously that the principle of Thought is what creates the entirety of our experience, but if you're anything like me, or the people I share this with, the magnitude of the implications of this truth just keeps expanding. As we see how the system works more clearly, we are brought closer to our deepest spiritual essence. Looking back on my experience in the Albert Hall, I can now appreciate that because of the outside-in misunderstanding, I had accumulated layer upon layer of unnecessary thinking – thinking about the difficulty of the music, judgements about myself, assumptions about my past and future, beliefs about how a violinist should sound, opinions about what success is, what health is, and what pain is. And those are just the tip of the iceberg. Included under the new paradigm's understanding of THOUGHT was also my entire felt experience, in other words, how the pain seemed to me, how important it was, whether I paid more attention to my shoulders than the rest of my body, not to mention my experience of my other senses – everything I saw in the concert hall, how the music and audience sounded to me, and how the air tasted and smelled. I still find it utterly mind-blowing that all these thoughts, bodily sensations, perceptions and judgements are only ever created from the same source – the formless principle of THOUGHT taking form in the moment – even though it often seems like they are coming from the outside world, a circumstance or a person. It appears to work one way but actually works another. This is the simple truth.

It is not yet commonplace for people to grow up with the Inside-Out understanding, so most of us are oblivious to the amount of THOUGHT-generated baggage we actually create and recreate, and just how much this can hamper us. You see, THOUGHT is a skilled illusionist whose job is to create an ultra-realistic experience, but if we don't know that it is the culprit, we will look in the wrong direction when we get stuck. As the physicist David Bohm said, 'Thought creates the world and then says, "I didn't do it".' The reason we can mistakenly believe that even one percent of our feelings can come from outside is precisely because THOUGHT is such a compelling storyteller or moviemaker. As soon as we start to look inwards for answers, it's just a matter of time before the made-up baggage starts to dissolve and our true essence shines through.

Subtractive Psychology, Not Positive Psychology

The paradigm shift that I am exploring with you here is disarmingly simple, but it has profound implications that make superstitious overthinking stop of its own accord. Instead of *adding* 'positive' thinking, tools or techniques – putting more on your mind – by contrast, it is understanding that relieves the mental noise, and excellence feels increasingly effortless as unnecessary thoughts dissolve on their own. This is subtractive psychology. Rather than unnecessarily tampering with the mind's 'computer' system, it's more about discovering the infinite flexibility and spiritual processing power that is always available. The question, of course, is 'How?' Quite simply, as we've been examining, it is about seeing through the illusion of the outside-in misunderstanding. This misunderstanding tries to tell us that something is lacking. It tells us we are separate. Understanding is about re-discovering how the mind truly works. Very often, when I'm not seeing things clearly, I catch myself and ask the question:

'Where do you think your experience is coming from?'

If it looks to me as though the feelings are coming from somewhere other than the principle of THOUGHT taking form in the moment, which I know is not possible, then I know I'm buying into the illusion. As soon as I realise that, something shifts inside me, and I feel increasingly connected to who I really am and with an innate sense of grounding, creativity and purpose. I'm not suggesting you ask that question as a tool to clear your mind, because, as I said before, this is not about 'doing', and there is no destination per se, but there is a lot to be said for looking in the right direction. When I was first learning about the Inside-Out understanding, I found it helpful that I was noticing just how much I had on my mind. In this chapter, I'd therefore like to challenge you to explore some of the places that THOUGHT might be hiding from sight.

Figure 7.1 shows a few examples of experiences that musicians have shared with me on gigs, in lessons, or in coaching sessions. What it highlights is the formlessness of spiritual energy compared to the fully formed products of the energy: namely, thoughts, beliefs, feelings, and experiences. You'll notice that as we head towards the truth of how the system works, everything gets simpler. Once we see that all problems only *look* like problems because of THOUGHT, a great burden is lifted, and the more clearly we see the implications in our own lives. We fall out of our thinking and into the infinite potential of the present moment.

Figure 7.1: Thoughts vs. Thought

'POSITIVE' THOUGHTS	'NEGATIVE' THOUGHTS	WHAT THOUGHT IS DOING
I am good at music.	I am not good at music.	I am judging and I am feeling my thinking, generated by the principle of THOUGHT in the present moment.
I am a good sight-reader.	I am a bad sight-reader.	
I am good at playing fast.	I am not good at playing fast.	
I can memorise music.	I can't memorise music.	
The bandleader likes me.	The bandleader doesn't like me.	I am guessing at other people's personal experiences of the world through the lens of my own personal experience of the world.
The musician is in the zone.	The musician is not in the zone.	
The musician is confident.	The musician is anxious.	
My idol never feels fear.	My duo partner always feels fear.	
The audience loves it.	The audience hates it.	

'POSITIVE' THOUGHTS	'NEGATIVE' THOUGHTS	WHAT THOUGHT IS DOING
I feel inspired.	I do not feel inspired	I am experiencing my body through THOUGHT in the present moment.
I have minor pain.	I have severe pain.	
I'm not worried about my fingers slipping.	I'm worried about my fingers slipping.	
This movement feels comfortable.	This movement feels unusual.	
The atmosphere is electric.	The atmosphere is dead.	I am having a sensory experience that only exists within CONSCIOUSNESS.
I feel a connection with the orchestra.	I feel disconnected from the orchestra.	
My mistake was not obvious.	My mistake was obvious.	
My instrument sounds good today.	My instrument sounds bad today.	

'POSITIVE' THOUGHTS	'NEGATIVE' THOUGHTS	WHAT THOUGHT IS DOING
Anyone can be a great musician.	Few people can be great musicians.	
Playing high notes is easy.	Playing high notes is difficult.	
My past is helping me.	My past is holding me back.	I am (re-) creating THOUGHT-generated beliefs in the present moment.
There is a correct position for the trumpet.	There is an incorrect position for the trumpet.	
I am not under pressure.	I am under pressure.	
This is a low-pressure gig.	This is a high-pressure gig.	

As we align our enquiries towards the spiritual truth of the Inside-Out understanding, we still have thoughts, feelings and experiences, but they stop controlling us as we realise they are being created by us rather than being inflicted on us. Because of the sheer amount of practice we have had at believing our thoughts, it can take time to shed superstitious thought baggage. Although this is a lifelong journey, each shift of perspective happens instantly. And a single insight can literally change the world. Deepening our understanding is always good for us. And it always spills over into the areas of our lives that need it most, be they our creative endeavours or not.

Even though we might not *enjoy* certain feelings, there are absolutely no rules about how we are supposed to feel. It is a myth that there are good emotions or bad emotions and that some should be chased and others should be avoided. In Figure 7.1, the first two columns aren't really 'negative' thoughts, or 'positive' thoughts. Strictly speaking, there's no such thing. They are simply thoughts. Judgement itself is a form of thinking that we are always free to relinquish. The human experience is natural and doesn't have to be resisted. You are allowed to feel anything. It's not so much that once we see that we work from the inside-out that we will never have feelings of performance anxiety, depression, procrastination, anger, or insecurity. What it means is that when we do have those feelings (and we will), we will no longer see a need to cope with them or fix them in any way. Why would we? The 'outside' world is effectively neutral because it's our own creation. Our feelings only ebb and flow within *us*.

Who Are You Really?

'So you're telling me that 100% of my experience is made up by THOUGHT?'

Yes, but it gets better than that. The 'you' who's having the experience is the same essential energy as the 'me' that's writing these words. Humans appear to be separate, but in fact we are united. This means there's way more depth to 'you' than you ever thought there was. Infinite, divine depth actually. You aren't your thoughts. Instead, you – the real you – is the energy that creates all thoughts, feelings and the way you experience all sensory data.

Figure 7.2: All made up . . .

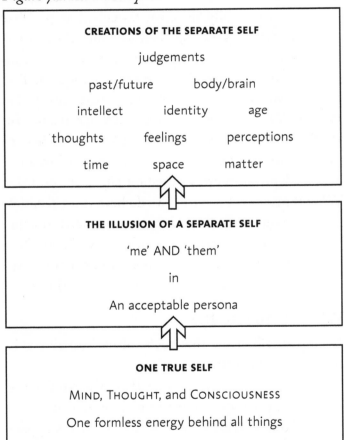

You are the capacity to have a thought, the ability to see things afresh, to have a change of heart, or to sing a different song. You, dear reader, are pure potentiality, which is why excellence is always on the table. It is innate. It is your deepest nature. You couldn't not be divine if you wanted not to be. As the superstitious thinking clears, who you really are becomes more and more obvious to everyone.

FORMED BY THOUGHT	EXAMPLES
What you think you are capable of.	'I won't become a top professional musician'. 'It's easier for her'. 'I can't have a day job and follow my passion'.
How you think about the future.	'Next year is going to be difficult'. 'It won't take long to get there'. 'I'll be happy when I've released the album'.
How you think about the past.	'I worked harder when I was a youngster'. 'I came from a musical family'. 'I can't be happy because of what happened'.

FORMED BY THOUGHT	EXAMPLES
What you think is possible or impossible.	'I cannot possibly learn to compose symphonies'. 'I can't memorise a whole sonata in a week'. 'Adults can't learn as quickly as children'.
What you consider easy or difficult.	'This concerto is difficult'. 'Playing a high C is risky'. 'All music is second nature to me'.
Whether you fit in.	'I don't belong in this band'. 'I need to leave'. 'I'm not built to play the violin'.
How important something seems.	'This is a once-in-a-lifetime opportunity'. 'I can't believe I blew the audition'. 'I *have to* warm up for thirty minutes before performing'.
The significance something has in your life.	'My shoulder injury is really holding me back'. 'Music is everything'. 'You're only as good as your last performance'.

FORMED BY THOUGHT	EXAMPLES
What you think success is.	'I didn't go to a proper music college'. 'I started at the age of three'. 'I've got the best instrument money can buy'.
How other people seem to you.	'He is doing well for himself'. 'She is a musical genius'. 'I'm always the slowest to learn new tunes'.
All thoughts about your identity.	'I'm not a songwriter'. 'Creativity is in my blood'. 'I'm a virtuoso'.
Expectations.	'I should be enjoying myself'. 'I should have mastered this by now'. 'Pianists should have long fingers'.

I often tell people that when they start to recognise THOUGHT for what it really is, it might actually make for a wilder ride, because instead of concocting an artificial emotional thermostat to prevent damage from unpleasant emotions, we understand that any temperature or intensity of emotion is actually totally harmless. So, instead of trying to upgrade our lives in an additive way, truth strips away contaminated superstitious thinking, revealing what was always underneath – the authentic self. That way we get to enjoy the whole rollercoaster ride with no censoring of emotions, no façade and no surplus thinking. We regain our childlike openness once more.

As a coach, I've had a great deal of coaching myself, and one of the unexpected benefits has been my health – especially my shoulder health. I gradually shed layers of old thinking about how I should be, about the limits I had placed on myself. I understood more about how THOUGHT functions, and I realised that my beliefs about posture and my shoulder-problem 'story' were merely creations. I lost a lot of fixed expectations of how I should hold a violin, of how I should carry myself, and about what was right or wrong. Spontaneously, I found myself looking for shoulder exercises that helped me, without the compulsion to try and feel OK. It suddenly seemed to matter a lot less. Once I started to release the need to control my experience, ironically, I felt more in charge. All the time I was suffering, I was only one thought away from a complete change of perspective, not to mention the wellbeing that we already all possess.

Chapter 7 Summary

MYTHS about who you really are

1. Some thoughts and feelings are good, and some are bad.

2. Some thoughts and feelings should be avoided, and others should be pursued.

3. If we have bad feelings, we risk losing something, such as 'reputation', 'self-esteem', or our 'identity'.

4. You are what you think.

5. There are rules about how the world is and how people should behave.

6. Shedding emotional baggage makes you a better, more-grounded person.

TRUTHS about who you really are

1. No thoughts are good or bad. THOUGHT is an impersonal energy.

2. We are always living in a subjective, psychological experience. Calling any thought positive or negative is just a judgement.

3. Who you really are is spiritual energy. *You* are not at stake just because you have bad feelings.

4. You are not your thoughts; you are pure CON-
   SCIOUSNESS.

5. People may agree on ideas, but at the level of
   principle there are no rules. Thoughts are form;
   THOUGHT is formless.

6. You are already perfect, whole, and complete. You
   are the formless, spiritual energy behind life.

EIGHT

WORKING 9 TO 5, WHAT A WAY TO MAKE A LIVIN'

LOST MUSICIAN: 'How do you get to Carnegie
   Hall?'
CAB DRIVER: 'Practise, practise, practise!'

This classic musical joke might sound flippant, but the underlying message is clear – more practice equals better results. But does it really? I've seen motivational mantras like 'practice doesn't make perfect – practice makes permanent' plastered on walls before, and this, just like the famous Carnegie Hall joke are part of a tangled ball of yarns that musicians have been spinning for many years.

So, what is mastery really all about? We've already seen how we're all spiritual equals and that the *capacity* to achieve excellence is innate, but what is going on with those who *actually do it* and reach the top of their game compared to the others who don't? Is it really

something available to all of us, or is there such a thing
as talent? Sure, there isn't a cookie-cutter approach
we can follow to get there, but if a deeper wisdom
is really guiding us in our practice, what can we do
to really listen to it in order to 'get to Carnegie Hall'
quicker? Let's take a look at mastery in more depth
and examine why the deeply embedded 'more is better'
approach to practice is so flawed.

The 10,000-Hour 'Rule' (That Never Was)

In 2008, Malcolm Gladwell suggested in his book *Out-
liers* that in order to achieve a world-class level of performance there was a magic number of practice hours
that needed to be completed. The '10,000-hour rule'
certainly has a nice ring to it, and it seemed plausible
enough on the surface, but it was a misinterpretation
of psychological studies and of how mastery is really
achieved. Gladwell's book cited a study undertaken by
Anders K Ericsson in which the amount of practice
undergone by various violinists was compared. One
conclusion of the study was that there was often a *correlation* between the amount of practice hours and the
level of expertise achieved. Other psychological studies
have also found a correlation between competition
success and amount of practice, but as I mentioned in
Chapter 1, there is a difference between correlation and
causation. And in the case of practice, it's an extremely
important distinction to get your head around. As
Ericsson's study and others have noted, expert musi-

cians develop their expertise by practising – a lot. And, to add credence to the 10,0000-hour rule, those who achieve better results in competitions or exams tend to have clocked up more hours of practice than those who don't. So, if this is the case, more practice must make for a better musician, right? Wrong, because the amount (and type) of practice that helps someone achieve a world-class standard of performance is a symptom of a state of mind, not a cause.

An easy way to illustrate this is with those strange moments that don't sit well with our 'more is better' mindset. When I was teaching violinists on the Junior Strings Project at the Royal Northern College of Music in Manchester, I often used to notice them get bored of their exam pieces in the run-up to an exam, but when we played them through for fun after a holiday or a break from playing, they would play the piece more musically than they had before, even though they were 'out of practice'. A similar anomaly will no doubt have cropped up in your own practice – if more is better, then why does practising for two hours a day not consistently achieve twice the result that practising for one hour does? And practising for six hours a day; six times the results, and so on? If time really is a causative factor and every hour is equal, why are some hours 'more equal than others'? The answer is because time is only a correlation, it's *not* a cause. The simple truth is that insight is the only factor that truly propels us towards mastery, but, of course 'mastery' is also a matter of opinion. Because each shift in CONSCIOUSNESS happens in an instant, how long you practise for is irrelevant compared to your clarity of mind when you practise. The principles behind the mind and peak performance are the causes.

Getting The 'Knack' – Insight, Not Hours

I was the type of child who loved to have new party tricks. It must have been the performer in me trying to get out. I learnt to pogo stick, to juggle, to make origami handiworks, to make all sorts of art projects, and I spent hours drawing and painting, not to mention learning to play various musical instruments. My father encouraged me to play the guitar, but then I went through phases of playing the mouth harp, violin, saxophone, tin whistle, bodhran, piano, drum kit, banjo; I even learned to circular breathe in order to play the didgeridoo. Later I picked up the cello, ukulele, clarinet and flute. Eventually, I settled on the violin and saxophone as my main instruments. Whenever I was frustrated by something, my mother would always say the same thing – 'there's a knack to it'. And I remember wondering what a 'knack' actually was. A knack is a hands-on, embodied understanding – a knowing. It is an insight, which is the true unit of practice, rather than the hour or the minute. It's very common to talk about practice in terms of units of time, but this is highly misleading. Anyone advocating 'practise, practise, practise' as the purest route to mastery has missed something fundamental about the nature of practice. We often ignore the central roles that a clear head and fresh insights play in mastering a skill, which is especially important if reaching an elite level of performance is your goal, whether it's in music, sport, or any other field.

Figure 8.1: A new definition

Insight (n.)

A spontaneous realisation that affects understanding, physical skill, or a person's psychological experience.

Synonyms: Get the hang of it. Get the knack. The penny drops. A shift. Get to grips with. Grasp something. To get it. To realise. To notice. To crack it. Pick it up. To learn. Nail it. Epiphany. Moment of inspiration. A brainwave. 'Aha!' moment. Eureka moment. Light-bulb moment. A breakthrough.

If a direct route to mastery is what you are after, then it goes without saying that you have to understand the rules of the game. One of the many reasons that the 10,000-hour rule was not really a rule was because each domain, be it playing the banjo, baseball, chess or learning Italian, has different requirements, and some domains involve many more 'knacks' to get than others. In addition to this, there are underlying principles behind learning each domain. Take for example how a bow makes a violin string vibrate. If you try to learn the violin repertoire by pushing the bow into rather than pulling it across the string to make a full sound, even if you practise for 10,000 hours, you will be working against the underlying principles of violin sound production, and therefore you will constantly be striving until the principles are grasped. The same can be said for how the body moves – bones, muscles, and tendons are arranged a certain way and thus certain movements are mechanically more efficient than others. Aiming first to understand, and then to *work with* the principles of the body will drastically improve the amount of fluidity, speed, and agility someone can achieve and will make a player less prone to injury. The central message of this book is that true underlying principles cannot be superseded, they can only be fought against or worked with. And of all such principles available, those with by far the greatest leverage are the principles of the human experience, because they underpin absolutely everything else.

Figure 8.2 Working with principles

TYPE OF PRINCIPLES	EXAMPLES	POTENTIAL CONSEQUENCES OF MISUNDERSTANDING
How the body works.	• The skeleton has a hip joint but does not have a waist joint. • Muscles themselves can only contract or release, they cannot push.	Injury, pain, inefficient movements, poor posture, loss of power, speed or agility.
How the instrument works.	• Clarinet tone holes need to be covered by the player's fingers. • Guitar strings need to be pressed firmly enough into the fret board to change the note and maintain a good tone. • Strength in the facial muscles is required to play certain wind and brass instruments with a good tone.	Poor sound, missing notes, difficulty playing.

TYPE OF PRINCIPLES	EXAMPLES	POTENTIAL CONSEQUENCES OF MISUNDERSTANDING
How the human experience works.	• The principle of THOUGHT generates all feelings, perceptions, and thoughts. • The variations and fluctuations of felt experience all take place within CONSCIOUSNESS. • We, like all things, are part of the same life energy that is MIND.	Far-reaching implications, including: unnecessary suffering (fear, anxiety, procrastination, depression, low self-esteem); unnecessary psychological effort (worrying, coping, being inauthentic); less-effective actions, decisions and decreased productivity.

One of the questions I asked at the beginning of the chapter was, 'Is there such a thing as talent?' In the context of this chapter, I'm not going to say that the only thing that will determine whether you achieve world-class mastery is your level of understanding of the principles of how the mind works. What I would say, however, is that a so-called lack of 'talent' is often used as a way of explaining away a person's misunderstanding of how the mind works. I'm prepared to accept that if you are five-foot-three you probably won't become the world's greatest basketball player, no matter how clear-headed you are; or, if you are six-foot-six, your chances of becoming a prize-winning jockey are slim to none. That said, apart from such purely mechanical considerations (and even those can be worked around as we shall see in Chapter 9), minor natural variations between people are far less important than we used to think. Often, the idea of talent is used to describe either someone who has already been on the path to mastery for some time, or someone who already understands something of how the mind works, before anyone had a chance to tell them that what they were doing was supposed to be difficult.

Let's take the example of a young musician called John. John doesn't seem very talented. He is nineteen and has just recorded a jam session of himself playing with other amateur musicians. His solo is disappointing because he frequently flounders over the basic chords. And he makes strange-sounding musical gestures where he attempts to copy some of the mannerisms of famous players, but his attempts just seem lukewarm and erratic. His sound is thin. The year is 1946, and the 'John' in question is John Coltrane. The session of him playing Tad Dameron's 'Hot House' is the first known recording of this jazz legend, made when he was in the navy. The reason I mention this is because Coltrane's dedication to practice would

become legendary among jazz musicians. He would
also be hailed as a genius, an innovator beyond compare, and a phenomenal 'talent'. And there are countless stories of him practising between sets at gigs, to a
roommate reporting he used to practise until his lips
bled, and to stories that he practised for so long that
he fell asleep with his saxophone.

Where does talent fit into this picture of a young
man at an early stage on the path to mastery? It doesn't
really, at least not in the sense that Coltrane had something that no one else can access. Just like any other
judgements of others or ourselves, talent and mastery
are in the eye (and ear) of the beholder. Coltrane could
reach an exceptional stage of musical development
during his lifetime because he took action on the
insights he had during his practice, which drove the
direction and the quantity of his practice. He chose a
ferocious pace *that made sense to him*, not because he
was told he should but because he wanted to. He felt
compelled from within. I'm certain, because of the
way that we all work, that he would regularly have
had times when he did not enjoy his practice, and that
he must have felt insecure at times – everybody does,
as we saw in Chapter 3. Understanding *this* deeply is
the key to reaching the highest levels of performance.
There is no doubt that he practised for a lot of hours,
but as a result of following his intuition, not to clock
up the time, or reach the magic 10,000. I'm also not
saying that he always did this, because I have no idea,

but the more deeply people see that their craft is 100% independent of their insecure feelings, the more readily they will take the action that intuition is suggesting.

Figure 8.3: Staying on the path to mastery

CIRCUMSTANCES/ FEELINGS	POSSIBLE CONSEQUENCES OF MISUNDERSTANDING WHAT YOUR FEELINGS ARE TELLING YOU DURING PRACTICE
Fear of sounding bad during practice.	• Only practising what feels good to practise. • Avoiding practising what makes sense to you out of fear of being exposed as a fraud or unskilled. • Practising to impress the neighbours or to satisfy the ego.
Fear of sounding bad in public.	• Turning down offers to play with other musicians, waiting for 100% certainty about how a performance will go. • Never performing a work in progress even if you know it could be a helpful experience.
Doubt about whether a teacher would be impressed by your best efforts.	• Putting off booking a lesson when you know it would be a good idea. • Avoiding practising so as to avoid feeling rejected by someone you respect had you given it your 'all'.

CIRCUMSTANCES/ FEELINGS	POSSIBLE CONSEQUENCES OF MISUNDERSTANDING WHAT YOUR FEELINGS ARE TELLING YOU DURING PRACTICE
Realising weaknesses in your playing that you know need addressing.	• Prioritising only the areas of your playing that are showing the most progress. • Practising the same amount you have always done in order to avoid too feeling obsessive.
Not feeling like practising.	• Only ever practising on days that you feel like it. • Trying to use mental techniques to feel motivated to practise.
Discovering that a famous musician played for fifteen hours a day when they were studying.	• Emulating the amount of time someone else practised without considering how insightfully that person practised. • Knowing it is time to stop your practice for the day but continuing because you feel it proves something about you.
Feeling insecure over whether you have enough talent.	• Only practising infrequently to avoid feeling 'untalented'. • Avoiding starting lessons for fear of feeling embarrassed or ashamed.

CIRCUMSTANCES/ FEELINGS	POSSIBLE CONSEQUENCES OF MISUNDERSTANDING WHAT YOUR FEELINGS ARE TELLING YOU DURING PRACTICE
Fear of failing.	• Not auditioning because of what failure would 'mean'. • Deliberately avoiding preparing as fully as you would like to.
Feeling bored of practising a particular passage or exercise.	• Using willpower to do a specific number of repetitions. • Stopping whenever you feel bored.
Feeling inspired by other musicians.	• Copying their habits, mannerisms, brand of equipment, etc, because you think it will give you something they have. • Only waiting until you are inspired before taking action. • Listening to certain music in order to get inspired, even when it doesn't feel right to do so.
Feeling intimidated by a person or a circumstance.	• Treating certain 'intimidating people' differently. • Preparing for 'big' gigs differently. • Assuming you need to do something to take your mind off a situation.

Figure 8.2 is not by any means exhaustive, nor do all of the examples necessarily apply to you, but it shows just a few common ways that the outside-in misunderstanding can take you on a detour from mastering your craft. The bottom line is that the more you act from an awareness of the Inside-Out understanding, the more likely you will feel connected to your inner sense of direction, and the less your progress will be inhibited by unnoticed overthinking. With a truer understanding of the mind as your foundation, working with the principles of how the body and how your instrument work can also speed things up considerably. To me, this is the number one reason why musicians should strongly consider getting not just a teacher who teaches about the instrument or the body, but also a coach who points them to the workings of the mind, because the potential to leverage everything else they do will be massive. The alternative, practising from misunderstanding and superstition, is an emotional wild goose chase, possibly harmful, and with no guarantee that you are targeting all your efforts in the right direction.

Chapter 8 Summary

MYTHS about mastery and skill acquisition

1. Progress is linear, measured in time or number of repetitions.

2. We are what we repeatedly do; therefore, consistent habits are essential to becoming a master.

3. Dedicated, disciplined practice makes you a dedicated and disciplined person.

4. Quantity and quality of practice matter.

5. Mastery is a destination that can be arrived at.

6. The purpose of feedback from a teacher is to pass on what they know.

7. It takes around 10,000 hours to reach a world-class standard of performance.

8. Talent is a rare natural gift that few are born with.

TRUTHS about mastery and skill acquisition

1. Progress is non-linear, measured by insight.

2. You are not what you do, and even within 'consistent' routines there can be mindless practice. Create the space for insight.

3. True dedication and discipline come from understanding, not from a routine.

4. Only the quality of practice matters. The right quality (ie state of mind) leads to the right quantity.

5. Mastery is a natural process that is never complete.

6. Nothing is truly 'taught', only ever learnt. The purpose of feedback is to draw out what you are capable of knowing.

7. It can take a lot more or a lot less than 10,000 hours to reach a 'world-class' standard depending on the domain and how rich in insight your practising is.

8. When a person works with the underlying principles of the body, the domain, and of how the mind works, they will appear more 'talented' because they understand the true nature of their task.

NINE

COME TOGETHER

'This whole show is about intimacy and connecting,
and I'm no different from anyone in this audience,
and they're no different from me; and I wanted it to
feel... real!'

Beyoncé Knowles, on her 2013 Las Vegas show

You and I both have something in common. Our
friends, acquaintances, and even the people we don't
like share it. This is something that everyone alive
today shares. Everyone who has ever lived has shared
it, and, if I may be so bold, it is not just something that
we share. It is something that we *are*.

In Chapter 2, we saw that everyone's mind works in
the same way – that there are principles, or psychological laws, that govern how all experience works. These
principles are beautifully simple, and most importantly
they are universal; they apply all of the time, to everyone. In Chapter 3, we explored the fact that every

person's experience ebbs and flows independently of
circumstance or perceived status. Chapter 4 took a
look at the difference between truth, which is permanent, and superstition, which is transient. We also
considered the cost of mistaking the two. Chapter 5
examined the innate capacity of every person to flourish and develop effortlessly. In Chapter 6, we looked at
how inner purpose is a powerful force of nature, and
it is always present. Chapter 7 showed that there are
no limits to what we are allowed to feel, nor are there
rules about what we should be feeling. Most recently,
Chapter 8 explored how understanding these principles is the single most leveraging factor when aiming
for mastery in music, sport or acquiring a skill. Each
of these chapters have been pointing to the underlying,
impersonal truth behind how human performance
works. As I said in Chapter 1, because it's impersonal,
this truth does not just apply to the field of music – it
applies to life as a whole. In this chapter, I'd like to
join up the dots and talk frankly about connection.

As musicians, we might feel connected with an
audience, an instrument, ourselves, or the music. That
said, while we might talk about connecting with an
audience, to a degree, we all love to stand out from
the crowd in some way. It could be a desire to be the
performer on stage, an urge to express our creative
individuality or to differentiate ourselves in some other
way, but many musicians' goals include an element of
distinguishing, or separating, themselves from others.

Being different can often be seen as a good thing, and ways to distinguish oneself – whether by being seen as naturally talented, as famous, as the hardest-working, as rich, as a 'creative person', as saying something original, as suffering for your art – can be used to distance ourselves in order, not-so-subtly, to say that we are more valuable, or dare I say it, *better* than someone else. The point is, however, we can't truly be better than someone else, because who we really are is *not separate*. Playing the tuba louder than someone else is possible. So is playing faster than someone else. But being better – whether that's morally, socially, spiritually or musically – just isn't a reality. That kind of comparison is purely a thought; it's not a truth. The same can be said of 'self'-improvement. But here's the thing, the idea that there is a separate self is a thought, too. It's a very helpful and highly practical thought to have, because this is how the world seems to us. And in the experienced world of form, we need to know whose legs to move to walk to the shops, or whose fingers to wiggle in order to write an email. But who we truly are is the spiritual essence. Not the body. Not even the personality. This spiritual energy is the real me, the real you, and the real *everything*. Being tricked by the illusion of separation, of duality, is necessary at times, but at others, forgetting it's an illusion can really weigh us down. The more you see this for yourself, the freer from effort your whole life becomes. Resistance to the illusion of duality, of separation, or of distinctions, is the essence of all suffering, and as the Sufi poet Hafiz said, 'Your separation from God, from love, is the hardest work in this world.'

You Don't Need To Try To 'Connect'

In order to connect two things together, there must be two separate entities in the first place. The simple truth, however, is that oneness ('connection') is already a fact. Our true essence couldn't be separate even if we wanted it to be. We are already part of the same, single whole. Our 'connection' to one another is already a pre-existing truth, because the spiritual energy of THOUGHT is the 'electricity' that powers all things. You simply cannot say that the electricity that animates your computer is any better or different to the electricity that brings your vacuum cleaner to life. The source is all the same. Though it can produce various outcomes, and it can be helpful or harmful, the energy itself only works in one fundamental way. It's the same with that which powers 'us' – our bodies may appear to be separate entities, and we have the power to create a vivid, personal reality, but the energy doing the creating is only ever one energy. It is the energy behind life.

When performers talk about their favourite performances, they often speak of having 'lost themselves', saying they felt 'at one' with the other musicians on stage or with the audience, or that they found themselves 'in' the music. As I've said previously, it can be

very tempting to make these kinds of flow experiences
into something mythical or extraordinary, but the
truth is that flow, an *experience* of the *fact* of oneness,
is entirely natural. It's quite normal. It's not important
whether we actually experience oneness all the time,
but it is important to be aware that the experience of
connection comes and goes, independently of circumstance. It is a harmless function of the principles of the
mind. The fact that you feel disconnected at times is
how it is supposed to be. Whenever these normal feelings
of distance, isolation, or exclusion subside, what we
start to notice again is the underlying 'connection'. The
pre-existing oneness. The divine. The god-ness that
resides within you. The god-ness that *is* you, in fact.
Now – and let me be clear – I don't mean God in a
religious sense here. I'm not talking about worship, traditions, or sacred texts. I simply mean the pre-existing
truth that both religion and science share. When sages
and wise teachers throughout history have told people
to look within for the answers, the 'within' they are
referring to is not within the body, or within the brain.
The truth is within life, within the moment – the real
you or true self – where all creations are forged. It is
a place of peace, of love, of humility, of authenticity,
and of pure potential.

Numerous traditions have their own ways of pointing to the truth of our spiritual oneness. In Sanskrit,
the word *namaste* is not just a greeting but in some
sense an acknowledgement of the divine in the person

that you greet. 'I bow to the God in you'. In Greek, too, the word *agape* is not just a love for another person, but a love for God, for humanity. The word *ubuntu* in the Zulu and Xhosa languages means 'I am because you are'. This spiritual fact, of course, is also something explored in music. From *alle menschen werden brüder* ('all men become brothers') in Beethoven's setting of Schiller's 'Ode To Joy', to the title of John Coltrane's 'A Love Supreme', the direction is the same – universal spiritual oneness.

The Illusion Of Not Belonging

When we realise who we really are – quite literally, the intelligent energy of life – then we start to experience the fact that we live in a world of abundance and can thrive anywhere. There is nowhere that you don't belong. You are always home. This might just seem like a nice idea, or it may seem obvious, or even ridiculous, but consider these statements:

- 'My hands are too small to play the piano'
- 'Women are not great guitarists'
- 'Those players are out of my league'
- 'Audiences in this city are always stone cold'

Each of these assumes that people can be divided into categories. Intellectually, of course, this is possible; but, in truth, someone with small hands, but who is in touch with an inner calling to play the piano, will find ways around the apparent disadvantage. There are plenty of extreme examples of musicians who weren't deterred, demonstrating that none of us need be. We each have the power to unwaveringly follow the direction of our hearts.

String players usually use the right hand to sculpt the sound with the bow, but Canadian violinist Adrian Anantawan was born without a right hand. Not only did he manage to learn to play using a prosthetic device, but he played so well he was accepted to study at the prestigious Curtis Institute, has made countless solo appearances, and is also now active as a teacher and as a public figure. Listening to Adrian play or talk about music, you cannot help but be struck by the fact that he has taken to music more than many people with two hands.

Another astounding story of belonging is that of Louisiana-born drummer, Dan Caro. When he was two, he toddled into his parents' garage and knocked over a can of petrol, the vapours of which were instantly ignited by a boiler pilot light. He suffered third- and fourth-degree burns over eighty percent of his body, and underwent many operations, losing both his hands in the process. Dan's inner flame burned brighter than the one that ravaged his body, and, amazingly, he found a way to express that. He learnt to hold and control drumsticks using elastic bands. And not just as a hobby but well enough to drum professionally. In addition, he is now an author and an inspirational speaker.

A final example of a musician defying expectations was the story of French virtuoso jazz pianist Michel Petrucciani. Michel was born with osteogenesis imperfecta, a genetic condition that meant he had brittle bones, had constant pain, and stood a little under three feet tall. Although physically it would seem he wasn't built for the piano – it was painful for him to play, and he was unable to reach the pedals – he became one of the most celebrated jazz pianists of his generation.

The illusion of separation will only hold back musicians if they mistakenly believe it is possible not to 'belong'. They will be more likely to see barriers than opportunities, barriers built on the illusion of the separate self, which doesn't exist. As these defiant musicians' stories prove, the energy of life can express itself, regardless of who we *think* we are. The principle of MIND offers everything we need – fresh ideas, universal wisdom, and the wherewithal to turn these into reality. So, you see, 'belonging' is the only way it ever really works.

Separate Realities

Though we are part of this one energy, the joke is that we use THOUGHT to have what seems like a unique personal experience. This means that everyone is walking around in a completely separate reality bubble to you. They generate theirs, you generate yours, and everyone's perceptual 'realities' are completely separate. What we *are* is one, but our *experience* can make us feel separate. This is a blessing and a curse – a blessing because we have a sense of responsibility over our body and the actions we take in the physical world, but a curse because we can easily be tricked into thinking that our experience of reality is the truth, or that our feelings are telling us about the world rather than about the spiritual energy that creates them. As you deepen your awareness of the Inside-Out understanding and turn away from the innocent misunderstanding, compassion will be the natural consequence.

The implications of separate realities alone are massive, but for the purposes of improving performance, let me simply say this: life is a relationship game, and so, too, is music. Whether it's getting the best out of yourself, the other musicians on stage, your students, your teachers, your family, your friends, your audience, your business, your management agent, your promoter, or your clients, understanding relationships will have a huge impact on your career, whatever stage you are already at. The only thing that really 'improves' relationships is seeing more clearly that other people are just like you because they *are* you. We act from the best understanding of reality that we have in any given moment, and the more we see our opinions about others as only that – opinions, rather than facts – the more curious we will become about their internal world. Once that happens, we have the greatest chance to impact people, not only with our music but with the course our life takes. Getting a gig, getting someone to pay you money for a product or a service, influencing a family member, passing an audition – all of these are *entirely* dependent on the other person's reality bubble, not yours. As *they* experience the connection with you, it all becomes easier. Conversely, the more our ideas, thoughts, or judgements play to the illusion of the separate self, the less likely we are to experience the connection that is there.

Experiencing Connection

The experience of connection and the fact of connection are not the same thing. To many, the ultimate performance is one where an artist seems to transcend the physical, and spiritual connection is experienced among performers, audience and composer. Yet it's not quite as straightforward as that, because all the members of the audience, although they are already connected to each other and might even all be having a good time, will experience the performance from within their individual reality bubbles. This is more good news because it makes it meaningless to try and impress an audience. Whether that happens is only ever up to each person's perception. That said, although we cannot *make* an audience member feel connected to us, somehow, our own sense of oneness has the ringing echo of truth about it – like the sympathetic resonance of one guitar string brought to life by another.

The more deeply at peace we are, the greater the chances of other people finding their own peace through our presence and through our music. It is as if we resonate at a frequency that is familiar. Because the two notes are really one, as one string sings its song, the other is reminded that it has the same song in it, too, and its song also begins to come out. This only happens if the string is allowed to vibrate – it cannot be clamped, muted, or dampened in any way. Thus, by having an open mind, in the broadest possible sense, we open our hearts to the infinite possibilities that exist – within the true self and within the moment. This is the ultimate consequence of a deep understanding of this whole paradigm, remembering that you are God. To me, this is the essence of music itself. Music is the song of humanity and also of God. This is the underlying reason why it is meaningless to say that someone has the secrets, or is more grounded, or wiser, or more 'talented' than you. Your true self is the true self of everyone else, the same universal energy source. So, by definition, you have enough talent, enough connection, enough wisdom and enough grounding. Truly, you do. You have everything you need, because you are everything.

Chapter 9 Summary

MYTHS about connection

1. You need to connect with an audience, a person or yourself.

2. Connection and oneness are just woolly new-age notions that don't help anyone.

3. Some people are better at connecting than others.

4. People, by their nature, are different from one another.

5. Thought, awareness, and God are completely unrelated.

TRUTHS about connection

1. We are all the same spiritual energy. The principle of MIND means that 'connection' is already there. You *are* other people, and they *are* you.

2. Considering the possibility that oneness is a fact and that the separate self is an illusion can reveal many profound implications.

3. Some of us rely on the fact of connection, others don't. But no one is more able to connect than anyone else.

4. The truth of connection is not the same thing as the felt experience of connection. You are one with the

universe even without experiencing it. THOUGHT, a universal intelligence, generates psychological realities that appear to be separate.

5. THOUGHT, awareness, and God are all one and the same. All languages, traditions and religions have their own way of pointing to this fact.

TEN

AND NOW THE
END IS NEAR...

*'Don't die with your music still inside you. Listen to
your intuitive inner voice and find what passion stirs
your soul. Listen to that inner voice, and don't get to
the end of your life and say, "What if my whole life has
been wrong?"'*

Dr Wayne Dyer

On my first visit to Russia, when I was dating Polina,
I visited the Novodevichy Cemetery in Moscow. The
cemetery sits next to a beautiful 19th-century con-
vent that is a UNESCO World Heritage site, and I
asked Polina to show me around because the cemetery houses the graves of some of the most famous
Russian musicians of the 20th century. I was looking
forward to seeing resting places of the composers
Dmitri Shostakovich and Sergei Prokofiev, violinists
David Oistrakh and Leonid Kagan, the cellist Mstislav

Rostropovich, as well as a clutch of other Soviet stars. It really was a who's who of top Soviet musicians. Bear in mind, this was Moscow in December. There was thick snow on the ground, most of which had been cleared by the maintenance staff, but finding the graves was numbingly cold, frustrating work. I was lucky to have a native Russian speaker with me, otherwise my chances would have been slim to none. Seeing Shostakovich's grave was my main reason for visiting Novodevichy. Ever since I had first played his symphonies as a violinist in orchestras as a student and learnt about the oppressive conditions in which he worked, I had adored his music.

When we finally found him, Dmitri's grave turned out to be modest and unassuming, unlike some of the enormous tributes elsewhere in the cemetery. I stood there silently, thinking that I was standing only feet away from a great composer whom I considered a genius. At that time, I took it for granted that he was a better man than me. He was more talented, had achieved more and was just made of different stuff. But then it hit me – I was alive, and he wasn't. I couldn't avoid the fact that he had been a human being just like me, and therefore had had his own insecurities. This was an insight for me at the time, and it was the first moment I'd ever really experienced a genuine human connection with a great composer. I found myself asking many questions: What is the point of striving for excellence if we're all going to die? To prove something? To whom exactly? To compete with others? If I 'win', then so what? To leave a legacy in order to prove something about my life?

I had been seeking musical excellence for many years, and this was the first time I had ever stopped to question why I was seeking excellence at all, something that would eventually lead me to question the need to seek outside myself at all. I didn't ruminate on this particularly, but I did return to it on and off for the next few years.

The best answer to this that I've heard was from the bassist Victor Wooten in a commencement speech he delivered at the University of Vermont. He simply said, 'What does the world need with just another good musician? What the world needs is good people.' The message of his speech was to live in a way that is authentic and that makes the world a better place, because there is ultimately no value (or need) to *prove* yourself to be talented or special. Ironically, understanding the futility of proving yourself means you're far more likely to impress. Anyone who has heard Victor play or has read his philosophy of music will know what I'm talking about. Now, I'm not saying not to work hard, cultivate your music or aim for perfection when you practise. But, although it might be appealing to compare yourself as one musician to another, or one set of achievements to another, ultimately, what are you actually comparing? One life's value with another's?

As we saw in Chapter 9, what creates 'you' also creates 'me'. Understanding – truly seeing through the illusion of separateness – reminds us that there is nothing to compare, nothing to fear, and nothing to resist. Understanding allows *all* our music to come out. We are inspired when something deep in someone else strikes a chord with something deep in us and draws out something that was dormant. Inspiration, originally, meant 'in spirit', 'divine guidance' – the 'breath of God'. As our personal thoughts get out of the way, suddenly the depth of what THOUGHT truly is reveals itself. In this final chapter, I will talk about getting your 'music' out, whether that is literally your music or the music that is you – your life.

Our Friend Slim

In 2016, I had the great honour of speaking at the funeral of a dear friend and mentor – a gentleman by the name of Adrian 'Slim' Hopgood. Slim was known for his larger-than-life personality and his not-so-diminutive stature, hence the ironic nickname. He was my music teacher, my school bandleader and an outstanding multi-instrumentalist. Over the years that he taught, mentored and supported me, we became friends, and I also got to know his family. Through Slim's encouragement, I started improvising jazz on the violin, and after catching the bug, I then took up the saxophone. This is part of the tribute I paid to Slim, standing beside his coffin:

Reading the tributes that were paid to Slim online from former Westbourne Jazz students like me, there was a common thread running through them all, and it was this – inclusion and connection. Youngsters felt safe in his presence, they felt valued and accepted just as they were. Lots of students mentioned how much of a sanctuary the school music rooms were for them, but it was not just a social club. All this meant something to us because, of course, it goes without saying that we all knew he was the real deal as a musician. I remember there was a time when it simply seemed like magic to me that he could play so many instruments. Looking back, I don't remember him playing his own instruments – we students were always cen-tre stage, but whenever he played a rare solo with Westbourne Jazz, which we all loved, he always used a student instrument – normally a flute or a sax. That meant a lot because it proved the magic wasn't coming from an instrument worth thou-sands, but instead it was coming from the music man. Maybe some of his magic had rubbed off on us, or rather the truth was that he was the magic, which meant that we were the magic, too.

As an angsty teenager, I remember playing sax on stage with him outside Christchurch Park in Ipswich one summer, and as he started off, I thought, 'I know I could do that one day soon.' But then as he let rip with some fast double-time flourishes, I realised that his playing was in a different league to ours. But there was no ego. He was so generous in letting us into his musical world. Whatever the occasion – a jam at a bar, a barbecue at school or at his house, a school concert after sixth-formers had already left, a gig he asked you to sit in on – the words were the same to people: 'bring your horn', 'bring your fiddle', 'sit in', 'get up and sing'. His love brought people together. And that, more than anything, is what I'll remember him for. His openness. It's also what I want to do more of in my life. When I heard that Slim was seriously ill, I was at the school at which I'm now head of music, and coincidentally the school at which Slim did his teaching practice. I was practising the sax, working on a tune called 'Red Clay', by Freddie Hubbard. In that moment, I realised my career, my instrument and my repertoire were all down to him. I was totally absorbed by the legacy of this man and know I always will be.

I started this book warning against confusing a symptom with the cause. I also said that this is not a book about music. Well, it's also not really about excellence, either. It's a book about life, because 'musical excellence' (whatever that really means) is a symptom of how you navigate your life. It's not a destination, and it's certainly not a cause. It is the sum of those actions, taken across a lifetime, that are grounded in how the human experience actually works rather than how it seems to work. Since my days in Slim's band, I've come to recognise that the qualities I remember in him are the same in anyone who has achieved a truly stunning level of performance. They seem to tap into their innate ability to be their authentic selves, and at an implicit level, they nearly always understand that however they feel in the moment, they can still take action. Actions that may feel scary, boring, impossible – whatever – but which are *required* by the moment. It is this freedom from circumstance and misinterpretation that enables them to keep doing what's right even when they don't feel like it. Understanding enables you to work on what you know needs to be practised rather than what you feel like practising. It also enables you to truly know that no person, opinion, or circumstance in the world could ever harm you psychologically. The principles are the cause, and what you feel in the moment is just one possible result. Whenever you see this truth instinctively, you are no longer able to take 'yourself' too seriously, because in that moment you insightfully see that there is no separate self. You're back home, and once again you see that life's a game to be played, exactly as a child does.

The paradigm I've introduced in this book, at the time of writing, is still in the early phase of its exploration and explanation, especially in terms of reaching musicians and performers. But there are green shoots of hope. Some truly outstanding work is being done by my colleagues who are sharing the three principles of MIND, CONSCIOUSNESS and THOUGHT, and if you haven't had the chance to yet, I wholly recommend you talk about this understanding with a teacher of it. What I repeatedly witness in people who are introduced to these principles is nothing short of a transformation. When people are put back in touch with their humanity, not only do they thrive and excel more consistently, but they experience more peace, fun and creativity; they enjoy happier relationships and have fewer anxieties. They use their time in a way that's more aligned with who they truly are. As we've seen, we can never stop having our ups and downs, of course (nor would we want to), but as we see fluctuations of THOUGHT for what they are, we make peace with the rollercoaster, the kind of peace a child has. And, just like that child you once were, you are now less prone to be tricked by the illusion.

Just Play!

The Inside-Out understanding is the single key to achieving your dreams. As you see for yourself ever more deeply that your feelings are totally independent of the circumstances of your life, and that your entire experience works from inside to out, not only are you truly free to take whatever action is necessary, but you can allow your light to shine so much more brightly. When we do that, as the author Marianne Williamson famously said, 'We unconsciously give other people permission to do the same.' Awareness of the principles of MIND, CONSCIOUSNESS and THOUGHT can render psychological suffering of all kinds obsolete. As we understand ourselves, in turn we understand others, and as a result, we do the thing that Victor Wooten pointed to. We make the world a better place, perhaps through our music, but ultimately because of who we truly are. War, famine, suicide, racism, and intolerances of all kinds have no place in a world that is awakened to the Inside-Out understanding – a world enlightened by love. When we insightfully see that neither circumstances nor other people can cause our feelings, then conflict and harmful behaviours will naturally recede. The greatest musicians that I can think of are the ones who have seen their potential to change the world, and who have given generously of the gifts they have within.

Don't take your 'music' too seriously.

It's not personal – it belongs to all of us.

You know what you're doing.

Just play...

ABOUT THE AUTHOR

Nick Bottini is a multi-instrumentalist, consultant and performance coach. Nick studied at Leeds University, the Franz Liszt Hochschule Für Musik in Weimar, and the Royal Northern College of Music in Manchester. He  has worked as a freelance musician, as well as Head of Music in London schools. As a workshop leader and public speaker he has shared the Inside-Out understanding of the mind with musicians, international sportspeople, business people and many others. For over ten years he has worked at various levels of the music industry from school children and adult beginners, to child prodigies, competition winners, music college students and top professionals. Nick lives in East London with his wife, Polina, and their cat, Kasya.

CONTACT

If you would like to learn more about the Inside-Out understanding, coaching, or upcoming events you can connect with Nick through the following methods:

✉ nick@nickbottini.com
🌐 www.nickbottini.com
🐦 www.twitter.com/nickbottini
📷 www.instagram.com/bottininick
📘 www.facebook.com/groups/justplaymusicians